Customer service in a competitive environment

Jon Passmore & Stewart Fergusson

Chartered Institute of Housing
Policy and Practice Series

The Chartered Institute of Housing is the professional organisation for all those who work in housing. Our purpose is to take a leading and strategic role in the encouragement of the provision and management of high quality, affordable homes for all. The Institute has over 12,000 individual members working for local authorities, housing associations, the private sector and educational institutions.

CIH, Octavia House, Westwood Way, Coventry CV4 8JP.
Tel. 0203 694433   Fax: 0203 695110

The New CIH Housing Policy and Practice Series aims to provide important and valuable material and insights for housing managers, staff, students, trainers and policy makers. The Editorial Team for the series is: General Editor: Professor Peter Williams; Series Editor: John Perry and Production Editor: Alan Dearling.

ISBN 0-901607-74-6

Customer service in a competitive environment
by Jon Passmore and Stewart Fergusson

Published by the
Chartered Institute of Housing © 1994.

Printed by Martins The Printers, Berwick upon Tweed.
Typeset by EMS Phototypesetting, Berwick upon Tweed
Designed by Alan Dearling for the CIH

Contents

ACKNOWLEDGEMENTS

The authors would like to thank the following people for their assistance with this publication.

General

Professor Peter Williams (University of Wales, College of Cardiff), Alan Dearling, John Perry (CIH) for steering this work to publication. April Knapp (Orbit HA), Peter Ward (Welwyn Hatfield DC), Susie Birch, Dr Andrew Thomas and Jane Boynton for their comments on the text.
Kay Clark and Val Tanser for typing the manuscript.

Chapter Information

Nina Dawes (Walsall MBC), Sarah Edwards (Derby City Council), Ewan Ramset (Aldbourne Associates), Tim Sewell (Wherry HA), Bob Rigby (Jersey City Housing Authority), Vaughen Lindsey (Shelter), Keith Williams (Islington LBC), Professor Robin Hambleton (University of Wales and previously of SAUS), Derek Campbell (Braintree DC), Wayne Hughes and Kevin Bentley (Focus HA), Professor John Hucket (Cranfield Institute of Technology).

Cartoons and Diagrams

Janet Matthews (Nene HA) for the cartoons. Open University and Professor Robin Hambleton for permission to reproduce diagrams.

The cartoons used in this publication are the copyright of Janet Matthews and must not be reproduced without permission.

This publication is dedicated to Victor Passmore and to Frank Fergusson.

PREFACE

Customer care may have become the fashion of the 1980s, but little lasting change occurred. With CCT facing white collar local government services and increasing Housing Corporation attention being placed on housing management, social housing providers need to act.

To be effective and create lasting change customer service needs to be seen as part of a broader pattern of management, which requires the bringing together of different elements into a coherent strategy.

This publication aims to provide an overview of customer service, at a practical level, but also explain the background and development of this new trend within social housing.

The book will be of interest to those who are currently working in the social housing field, either in the voluntary or statutory sector. We also hope the book will provide useful information to those undertaking qualifications; BTEC, diploma or graduate level within housing, surveying and local government administration fields.

The publication is divided into eight chapters, which consider the pressure for change, managing the process of change and the outcomes good practice organisations have achieved.

The book's structure aims to allow the reader either to dip into individual chapters for detail about a specific topic, or to read the book sequentially to develop a broad understanding of customer orientated services. Chapters One to Six were written by Jon Passmore and Chapters Seven and Eight by Stewart Fergusson.

CHAPTER 1: CUSTOMERS AND CHANGE

Introduction

This chapter aims to:

- define the use of the term 'customer'

- explain the misunderstanding and misuse of customer services in the 1980s

- explain the relationship between change management and customer service

- offer a model to analyse the external competitive environment which social housing organisations operate within.

Who Are Our Customers?

There is considerable debate about the use and misuse of the terms 'customer', and customer service strategies. The use of the term in this publication is sharply defined, which takes the definition at its broadest building in not only those that can exercise choice – like the supermarket shopper – but those with expectations about the organisation and its performance.

The expression 'customer' is a relatively new word to social housing providers. Local government, in particular, but also housing associations have managed to exist without recognising that the tenants and applicants with whom they dealt were customers who had rights and expectations. In more recent years there has been a recognition that 'customers' exist, but in many organisations there has been little practical change in the way services are delivered.

If consideration has been given to the concept of the 'customers' it has generally been in the limited definition of those who receive services directly from the organisation; tenants, homeless people and housing applicants. However, a broader deinition may be of more value and enables the wider 'stakeholders' to be built into a model of service provision. The inclusion of 'stakeholders', not necessarily users, but those who hold expectations about the organisation, broaden the limited definition of customer. This secondary group of customers includes; employees, the Department of the Environment, the Housing Corporation, local Councillors and M.P.s, plus a host of other agencies.

This recognition of a wide variety of customer groups also brings a need to recognise the varying interests and priorities which these stakeholder groups hold, and which frequently conflict with one another, as they occasionally do within individual groups. For example; two tenants may be seeking a transfer to the same house. It is impossible to satisfy both demands. Alternatively a local councillor and the local M.P. may wish to see more building of council homes, but the Department of the Environment favours housing association provision on the site.

The issue is further complicated within the public sector as some service users may be 'unwilling customers' of the service. The classic example is the prisoner, who is an unwilling consumer of Her Majesty's Prison Service. Housing too has unwilling consumers. In the case of a local authority, an individual served with a closing order or repair notice on an unfit property, is unlikely to be satisfied or 'delighted' by the Council. Housing association tenants in arrears are unlikely to welcome the association's rent collection service.

Other groups too may either be unwilling or at least unwitting consumers of a service. These customers may be unable due to illness or disability to make informed choices about the services they receive. Some customers of sheltered housing or enhanced care schemes provided by some associations may be included here. The dilemmas which face public organisations are most acute in the NHS. Work undertaken by the King's Fund Centre on priority care groups in the NHS has emphasised the value, needs and rights of the individual receiving primary health care. Other organisations (NCVO 1984) too have focused attention on client dignity. These themes have been picked up by the Patients' Charter.

From our discussions it is clear that the term 'customer' can be used as a collective term which brings together various groups of stakeholders. It is this wider definition which we intend to use for this publication; a customer is:

"an individual or organisation who receives benefits from, or holds expectations about, an organisation and its performance."

A Narrow View of Customer Service

Few organisations have escaped the growing trend to adopt 'customer care', but of them, very few have adopted the approach as a philosophy which underpins the delivery of services. More commonly, misconceptions have grown up in social housing, restricting and limiting the movement towards empowering customers, particularly groups whose voices are rarely heard. A consideration of these misconceptions can enable both a clearer understanding of what is meant by 'customer services' in this publication and will ensure that those who argue that "customer service is not relevant here" or "yes, we are a customer care organisation already" can begin to explore the value of broadening a customer services approach from the tactical towards the strategic. There are perhaps three common misconceptions.

Misconception 1 – 'We are already caring for our customers'

Organisations and their employees nearly always believe they care for their customers. Sometimes this is out of a sense of loyalty to the organisation, but more often paternalistic care becomes confused with service quality. The higher up the organisation's hierarchy one travels, the greater the gap between perceived care and service reality.

Probing these managers to discover what their views of customer satisfaction are based on reveals some interesting assumptions. Managers frequently quote evidence of good practice or innovation. While innovation needs to be encouraged such initiatives may fail to generate significant change in patterns of provision. Refurbishment of a reception area does not create a customer services organisation, unless this change is supported by a programme of training for front-end employees and an organisational review of service delivery. Unfortunately such beliefs in overnight change can regress from innovative excellence to simple changes in management practice. These changes may not have any significant benefit to customers. Managers often refer to sending an acknowledgement card to correspondence from customers as a positive example of customer care. More worrying was the authority whose best example of customer care which a senior manager could think of was the corporate tie.

Misconception 2 – 'We must train our receptionists in customer care'

If social housing providers do decide to positively pursue customer service this frequently starts at the 'front end'. Customer contact staff are provided with training in dealing with the public, but this recognition of a need to improve customer service does not flow through other aspects of the organisation's operations. This approach is based on a belief that if you get the employees who deal with the public to treat them nicely, customers will be satisfied. This belief is naive, and rather than improve services, is only likely to exasperate customer-organisation relations.

Those responsible have failed to consider the chain which links customer contact employees at the reception through the organisation via policies, procedures and support staff to the underlying culture of the organisation. If the culture is one of 'don't care', training reception employees to smile will bring few benefits, and can send a negative but often unintentional message which can actively work against change. When devised by senior managers and targeted towards customer contact employees, the programme can send a message which employees read as, 'You have failed in your job to look after the customer, now we as managers have to come in to sort out the problem'. Few employees will be motivated to deliver a fresh and dynamic service in the light of feedback from managers which concentrates on failure and shifts the blame to the customer contact employee. The likely outcome is a mechanistic delivery of 'have a nice day', which is so familiar in those organisations which are trying, but failing, to deliver the caring service which managers in the organisation desire.

Misconception 3 – 'Customer care is a good idea, but ....'

This misconception usually continues with one of several lines – 'we frequently have to say no to our customers', alternatively employees say 'it won't work here'.

This view is often underpinned by the belief that customer service is solely about saying 'yes'. This is untrue.

In areas where resources are limited, and which have a wide variety of stakeholders, it is inevitable that some customers will be adversely affected by any decision. The application of customer care to this area should not be seen implicitly as always meeting customer demands but rather managing the customer interaction. This ranges from setting expectations about the quality and content of service to delivering the service sensitively to individual customers. This management process is complex and can involve a new approach for many social housing providers. It is this management process, the mechanisms for analysing this management of the customer interaction, and techniques and problems of implementation which we will concentrate on later.

The Need for Customer Service

While organisations continue to struggle to come to terms with the concept of service users as customers and the potential impact on service delivery this brings, the need for change remains strong.

Local government is threatened as services are shifted towards the centre and as central government promotes greater competitiveness within housing. If local authorities do not provide the quality of the services to customers at the right time and at the right price, direct services provision may be lost. This reduces local authorities to a strategic role, weakening local democracy and strengthening the argument for abolition of local government tiers, restructuring or removal of services by statute.

For those exposed to the competitive environment, customer service offers a potential tool for generating competitive advantage (Passmore 1992). While it may be difficult for local authority direct services to compete purely on price, authorities which play to the strengths of their DSO can bring benefits to customers and enable in-house bids to compete with external competitors who may be less well tuned to customer demands or lack the trained team orientated staff to ensure standards can be maintained. The client by writing a specification which is customer focused may not only protect service standards, but play to the strengths of the organisation's experience in delivering this type and standard of service quality.

Equally, if not more, important is the threat to resources. While organisations may face the challenge of CCT, the reduction or reallocation of resources is a major threat facing all public services. In local government the threat of local government review, brings with it a threat of abolition for the smaller district councils in England. This is forcing authorities to look again at community partnerships, links with parish councils and focusing services at customer needs. The housing association movement, with Corporation monitoring and local authorities becoming more demanding in terms of housing management standards, has forced associations to consider the needs of its tenants.

The ability of an organisation to meet these demands depends on the skills of its employees to deliver at the point of contact with the customer a unique combination of different elements.

Each customer may have their own priorities, the only person who can know what is required at the time is the person serving the customer. That employees must bring together their knowledge of the organisation's mission and strategy, use effective communication skills, detailed knowledge about the customer's query plus accessing information through IT or other systems, to sell to the customer a response to their question which the customer understands and is satisfied with.

Social, Technical, Environmental & Political (STEP) Analysis of The Social Housing Environment

The second part of this chapter considers the issues which influence the social housing environment. A simple model can be used to carry out an analysis of any organisations competitive environment. The STEP model analyses the competitive environment under four headings; Social, Technical, Environmental and Political factors.

Social	Technical
Political	Economic

The social housing scene has been affected by an array of individual factors. It is these factors which lend support to the arguments for continual review of organisational policy and practice, but have also lead to the notion of customer service.

Social Factors

A broad range of social change is taking place within British society; changes in employment patterns, privatisation, a movement away from a collectivist approach to individualism and growing expectations about personal prosperity. The latter of these is in part a factor which has contributed towards the drive for customer services, as social housing providers attempt to respond to consumer pressure.

Directly within the social housing field, the growth of individual rights under the 1980 Tenants' Charter has been complemented by the 1990s Citizens' Charter. While the Council Tenants' Charter launched in 1992 offered no new legislative rights of direct value to tenants, it set out standards of good practice, which could be of practical benefit to local authority tenants.

The growing recognition of equal opportunities has impacted on providers with a code of good practice published by the Commission for Racial Equality, but also positive action in training and by encouraging the development of black housing associations, through stock transfer and development agreements with larger associations.

Changing social patterns may include:

* impact of European Community employment rights – TUPE
* continued demographic and gender change in employment and housing demand
* growing individualism
* growing tenant expectations.

Technological Factors

Growth of the green movements (Friends of the Earth) has brought technological issues back onto the housing agenda, after the demise of system build. Technology is being used in new ways to measure the thermal efficiency of housing. National Home Energy Rating (NHER) and Starpoint offer schemes to housing developers and providers to measure the efficiency of individual homes and offer solutions to reduce heat loss, through double glazing, cavity wall fill, loft insulation and heat exchangers.

In the office environment the continued development of IT means greater sophistication. Systems which will allow housing benefit calculation in tenants' homes and automatic cash payment machines which collect rents around the clock are available and are being increasingly used by social landlords.

The likely issues for the 1990s could include:

* environmental policies
* information technology
* communications.

Economic Factors

Economics have impacted on social housing to possibly the same extent as political factors, changing the shape of provision. An analysis of tenures reveals how subsidy has been targeted during the 1980s towards the preferred tenure of owner occupation. This has occurred at the expense of other tenures, which have failed to receive the level of subsidy and tax relief which owner occupation has benefited from. The 1990s continue to see a growing shift in resources, targeted towards need.

Wider economic forces at the turn of the decade drove interest rates high, resulting in the eviction of many people who had bought during the boom years of the late 1980s. This served only to exasperate the homelessness problem, which has been continuing to grow since the economic problems of the mid 1970s.

The 1990s will continue to demand change from those in social housing. The key issues which may affect those in housing during the 1990s are summarised below:

* changing financial regime
* subsidy withdrawal from new build
* cost management for the housing CCT environment.

Political Factors

Social housing has been a political football, which neither major party has grasped and decided to run with for the benefit of tenants. Policies have often been the outcome of a search for economic benefits, or central government desire to break up the monopoly of large Labour controlled landlords. The 1990s are unlikely to see a significant change in this process, social housing providers and managers will be expected to perform a juggling act.

Political factors arguably have had a major impact on the social housing movement, and can be expected to continue to do so, requiring change from providers to meet the changing policies, funding arrangements and legislation. The issues for the 1990s may include:

* Citizen's Charter and customer contracts
* tenure transfer – Right to Buy
    – Rents to Mortgages
    – Voluntary stock transfer
* competitive tendering
* declining public funding and growth of private finance.

Managing Change

With the changes we have described in the STEP model, an understanding of the factors which underpin the changing environment is the first step in beginning to manage the change process. Without such an understanding of the issues, change management often becomes responsive and incremental, as individual issues develop and recede. An alternative which this publication advocates, is proactive and strategic management, tackling issues through consistent and integrated policies, which are linked to clearly defined and published mission statements and which are customer focused.

This process of 'crafting change' relies heavily on an interaction between the organisation's managers and its customers. Managers, aware of the changing environment need to look to customers for options and solutions. It is this process of consulting, listening and responding which forms the core of customer service strategies.

Summary

- The term customer is misused and misunderstood. We have defined the term as "an individual or organisation who receives benefits from or holds expectations about an organisation and its performance".

- In applying customer service during the 1980s, organisations have applied a series of misconceptions which have limited the application of customer service to a tactical level.

- The growing competitive environment of social housing demands greater customer focus to survive or gain competitive advantage.

- To apply customer service strategically demands that managers manage change and understand the forces at work in their environment.

- The STEP model offers a tool to analyse the competitive environment.

CHAPTER 2:
HOUSING UNDER PRESSURE

Introduction

This chapter aims to:

- Identify and analyse the main features behind the growing competitive environment in social housing.

The Need for Change

Housing is under pressure to change. Consecutive Conservative Governments during the 1980s felt public housing formed part of the 'nanny' state which had developed since the war, and attacked it with a vigour few could have imagined possible in 1975 when council housing was at its zenith. During the years which have followed, council housing starts have fallen from an annual out turn in excess of 100,000 units to a mere trickle. A million and a half homes have transferred tenures, the majority to home ownership under the Right to Buy, but an increasing number through large scale voluntary transfer and trickle transfers.

While council housing has been in decline, the housing association movement has tried to rise to the challenge offering a new dawn of social housing. However its response to housing need and management practice has failed to live up the the promises made. Associations are under pressure from the Housing Corporation to change old management practice. Performance monitoring has become more vigorous and development funding now follows the Associations which 'perform'.

With a major stake in social housing, government pressure has shifted towards local authorities management track record. Legislation has enforced performance monitoring and funding is being used to encourage performance improvement.

Internal pressures from politicians, professionals and employees remain, and in the former case have become pronounced as external political pressures grow.

Tenants' Choice

If a single trigger which stimulated interest in customer service could be identified, the Housing Act 1988 is it. Part IV of the Act introduced a right for tenants to effectively opt out of local authority control selecting their own landlord through a ballot. The opt out, however, was one way, and while developed as a mechanism to encourage tenants' individual choice, it was perceived as 'an alternative landlords charter' for take overs. This local authority interpretation developed due to the unusual ballot procedures adopted for the legislation. The procedure could be initiated by the approved landlord listing the properties where they wished to consult tenants about opting out. A process of consultation would be followed by a ballot in which, to stay as council tenants, tenants had to vote positively for their local authority. A failure to vote was seen as a positive vote for a transfer and would result in the approved landlord taking control.

As a few housing associations proceeded to apply and obtain approved landlord status, Tenants' Choice became 'Friday 13th' for the council tenants of Elm Street. Like most movie-horror shows, the anticipation of the murder has been worse than the event. In fact, all large Scale Voluntary Transfers – LSVTs have been initiated by the local authority and only a small number of tenant lead Tenants' Choice ballot on individual estates have taken place, despite fears in 1987 that Tenants' Choice would result in active private landlords bidding to take over council estates.

The fear which developed among local authorities in 1987 following the publication of the bill has not disappeared, although for most it is more of a spectre to be conjured up either to stimulate member support for an LSVT or other management initiatives. Virtually every authority has in response adopted 'customer care' as a means to promote tenant loyalty. The reality of such strategies has been in the main farcical, offering little more than gift wrapping to elected members from senior managers out of touch with what customer contact staff and tenants want to see.

Citizens' Charter

The Major Government has brought with it a notable shift in emphasis, away from challenging local authorities because they are part of the public sector, towards encouraging greater accountability and stimulating value for money.

The core of the Citizens' Charter has been 'passengers, patients and parents' (HMSO 1991). However, the programme has touched virtually all public services. The White Paper was launched in 1991 followed in 1992 by the Council Tenants' Charter. This was a follow up to the original 1980 legislation which gave Council tenants security of tenure.

Four main themes run through all of the charters; quality, choice, standards and value. These are underpinned by a set of principles which citizens are entitled to expect, first expressed in the original Charter (HMSO 1991):

  * standards
  * openness
  * information

* choice
* non-discrimination
* accessibility
* redress.

Explicit standards should be published by each service provider, and be available to all users. The standards should include helpfulness, statutory times and waiting times. The organisation should monitor its performance and report to customers on progress. A failure to achieve a target should not, however, mean targets should be reduced.

The Charter encourages greater openness in public services. Information should be available on who one sees, who's in charge and what is the cost of the service.

Further, the information which is provided should be in plain language, and be comparable between different authorities/associations and over time.

Citizens should be provided with choice where this is possible. In many aspects of the service, such as whom a tenant's landlord is, real choice is not available. Swapping landlords is not as easy as changing washing powders. However users should as a minimum be consulted about changes and have a right to participation in the management and have elected representatives.

Equal opportunities should be a consideration of public services, according to the Charter. In Wales the Welsh language should be used in addition to English. Where there is a clearly identifiable ethnic group, information should be made available in ethnic languages, plus monitoring of service delivery.

The issue of accessibility is a right which consumers should expect. This means flexible opening hours, telephone enquiry points and accessible buildings.

Finally, citizens are entitled to expect an apology and an explanation if things go wrong. A well publicised and straightforward complaints procedure should be available. The priority should be towards improving services, rather than offering compensation schemes.

In the housing sector the 1991 White Paper offered a hint of the changes to come:

* improved Council Tenants' Charter
* greater rights for tenant self management/ownership
* stronger tenants' Guarantee
* CCT for housing.

The commitment for local government was limited to offering an extension of CCT to white collar services.

The Charter presents a major dilemma for local authorities, if not for associations. For local authorities the conflict is between driving up quality through a requirement to set standards, publish information, monitor performance and put right mistakes, while also achieving value for money demanded by capping and CCT.

The first objective may be applauded by all, the second is of questionable merit. Critics argue the CCT regulations prevent DSOs competing on a level playing field. Further, the task of defining personal services is more complex than manual services, which may lead to a fall in standards if contracts fail to define clearly and precisely the services required.

More recently the principles of the Charter have been refined to:

* standards
* information and openness
* choice and consultation
* courtesy and helpfulness
* putting things right
* value for money.

The cost of the Charter initiative has been high. For 1992/93 an estimated £0.75 million was spent producing publicity material on the initiative by Government departments. Implementation costs are unquantifiable across the range of public services included in the initiative.

Further expenditure is planned with the launch of Citizen Charter hotlines, which are estimated to cost £1 million. These provide citizens with freephone information about the Charters which are available, opting out and other related Charter proposals.

Competitive Tendering

CCT for housing management, introduced under the Leasehold Reform, Housing and Urban Development Act 1993, has brought a new force stimulating change. The success of CCT in government terms has been its reduction in costs and removal of union influence in the manual sector as private firms win tenders. Both achievements are contested by opponents of CCT who argue contract monitoring has forced total costs up even if slight reductions in service contract costs have been achieved. Service standards have fallen and any gains that have been made are at the expense of low paid workers, most often women.

The concept was first mooted by John Major in advance of the 1992 election and it was suggested by housing commentators that either the government would not proceed as CCT in white collar services offered few benefits and was highly complex and, secondly, like tenants' choice, it would have no real effect in changing patterns of provision. In hindsight both propositions have turned out to be wrong.

The legislation, along with detailed regulations, are in force and authorities are implementing the Act. Restructuring of departments into 'client' and 'contractor' has taken place. Contract specifications have been produced with help from professional bodies such as the Association of District Councils (ADC) and Chartered Institute of Housing (CIH), who have published a good practice guide on housing CCT (ADC/IOH 1993). While it is impossible to deny the task of contract specification has been more complex than refuse collection or housing repairs, contracts have been produced and let. The effect too has been real. In Rutland, the housing department disappeared to be replaced by a private contractor even before the legislation was enacted. While Rutland may be seen as a special case other authorities have also pursued this route, to gain the advantages of voluntary tendering.

Housing consultants and associations have seen CCT as a route to a new business. For associations no longer acting as developers, CCT does offer a potential route for growth. A successful contract could lead to a stock transfer and a number of authorities sponsoring their own associations, either independently or as part of a wider group structure, see the contract management as a first step along the road of winning tenant support for the new organisation.

For authorities who wish to retain services in-house, customer service strategies offer one route to retaining services. Past experience of service provision and a close working relationship between client and in-house contractor can enable a specification which plays to the in-house contractor's expertise to be produced and which emphasises high standard of service delivery.

Funding Performance

For associations, the increasing focus on performance has encouraged a change in attitudes from the old Housing Association Grant (HAG) regime of the 1980s to the mixed funded regime of the 1990s. Some commentators believe the change has corrupted the voluntary housing movement with too great a focus towards business management and insufficient attention towards need and caring: the social worker being replaced by the accountant.

Under the new regime, funding is increasingly following performance, assessed during Corporation performance audits on a range of criteria:

* committee and management control
* financial management
* access to housing

* housing management
* property maintenance
* development.

Further, it has been suggested that associations should no longer be involved in development but rather buy the product from developers or that development should be restricted to a dozen or so major associations. In this way greater value for money could be achieved.

The focus on development costs has unfortunately overshadowed management issues which have taken a back seat in the monitoring process. The possible exceptions to this have been equal opportunities and tenant participation. The issues of customer orientation and accountability have been weakly grasped by the association movement. Customer groups wider than individual tenants, such as applicants and relatives, have generally not been considered. Among the broader groups of stakeholders, local authorities and citizens, few associations have opened their doors to listen to the views of these groups and how the association can adapt to meet community needs more effectively.

Housing Investment Programme (HIP) — Allocations

Unlike Housing Association Grant, HIP allocations of Basic Credit Approval (BCA) and Supplementary Credit Approval (SCA) have increasingly focused on management issues. Performance was unimportant when allocation was based on the housing need measured by Housing Needs Indicator (HNI) and when little data was available to compare performance. Both of these factors have changed.

The 1989 Local Government and Housing Act introduced a requirement for authorities to collect and publish a detailed range of performance indicators (Passmore 1991 a & b). While initially resisted by authorities as a waste of effort, publications have become increasingly sophisticated, although it is acknowledged tenants do not fully appreciate the quality of data produced (CURS 1992). More recently, the Citizens' Charter indicators collected by the Audit Commission, now require the majority of local authority services to publish performance standards in the local press. Housing is included among the list of services for which data must be produced. The requirements for the Audit Commission however do not mirror the requirements under the 1989 Act.

As a result of the Audit Commission Shaw Classification comparison between authorities is possible, although is of questionable benefit. In practice the Shaw Family groups are disregarded and local papers and the Department of the Environment alike compare neighbouring authorities even if their housing stocks and social problems differ widely.

The second change which has stimulated improved performance is the shift away from allocating resources purely on need towards performance allocations. Currently 60% of the capital allocation is based on performance, which considers:

* strategy
* programme
* enabling
* management
* tenant participation.

In the development of the overall strategy, consultation is seen as important. The DOE encourages authorities to involve all potential stakeholders and to reflect their comments in the final document. The presentation too should be a public affair, and consider the total needs of housing within the district.

The second area of assessment, programme delivery, focuses on the ability to spend up to estimates, value for money achieved within the programme and flexibility in responding to investment opportunities.

Enabling has taken on greater significance during the 1990s. Authorities are expected to co-ordinate social housing provision in their district. These may include the use of planning powers, grants to associations and private landlords, stock transfer and private sector housing initiatives, such as flats above shops.

The fourth area of management concentrates on performance indicators, homeless policies and maintenance planning. The indicators required under the Housing and Local Government Act however, fail to consider tenant satisfaction or a landlord's efforts to encourage participation. This is covered in the final section. Authorities are expected to show that they monitor customer satisfaction regularly and provide choice in modernisation. For urban authorities, Estate Management Boards, Co-ops and other tenant initiatives are encouraged.

The shift in the DOE position has been marked, as early evaluations failed to consider tenant needs. There is still concern expressed that little weight is put on tenant initiatives, unless these provide a mechanism for self management or movement away from local authority ownership.

Internal Pressures

Internal pressures too have been at work encouraging social housing providers to consider the needs of their customers more explicitly. Three individual factors may be identified; political, professional and employees. As with external pressures these have not operated in isolation, but have combined with or are the outcome of other factors, some of which have already been identified in early chapters.

Political pressure among left wing Councils attempting to pressure and enhance local government and political power have been a major force, as have efforts by a select band of Conservative controlled councils trying to enhance the business management of their organisation of which they saw customer orientation as a key feature.

The Left's early efforts were more concerned with decentralisation. While authorities such as Leeds' had retained a decentralised approach for decades, the majority of metropolitan and district councils had centralised in the 1970s into the town hall. The 1980s saw this trend being reversed, first and most prominently at Walsall (Seabrook 1984), but gradually neighbourhood housing offices were spreading like pizza huts through the London Boroughs and urban authorities. Neighbourhood housing offices offered the potential for service improvement, and while the capital costs of moving out of the town hall were high and revenue costs often rose as the service became more accessible, the success of decentralisation as a strategy is generally acknowledged.

Under growing pressure from resource cuts and Tenants' Choice, the second wave of service enhancements followed from a mix of Labour controlled councils; York, Welwyn Hatfield and Leicester, and London Boroughs like Lewisham. Here efforts to inject market standards through customer contracts were pursued (Berry 1991), along with customer care codes and complaints procedures to enable customers to understand what they could expect and, if things went wrong, how mistakes could be put right. While not stated, the hidden objective was to assist local government in general and housing in particular, to fight back. An argument was advanced of service users understanding what services were provided and why these were being cut back; this information may affect voting patterns at the national level. The 1992 election revealed the weakness of this argument. Customers, however, benefited from the service improvements which took place, and saw Labour initiatives adopted by John Major as his big idea – Citizens' Charter.

The efforts of Conservative Councils continued on a smaller scale and were less concerned with the national agenda and more with the concept of the enabling council. They argued that by splitting service operation from service policy, each manager could focus more effectively on their individual task. Not surprisingly, the most successful councils in the customers' eyes, measured by independent surveys such as MORI, have been those that retained services in-house, such as Braintree. While distinguishing between strategy and operation, they actively intervened, and relied heavily on surveys to set standards and measure success, as well as investing in training and corporate planning to maintain future momentum. Like the Labour Councils, these Conservative authorities believed local government had a key role to play in the local community, and the customer needed to know and understand that role.

The second pressure factor within housing has come from professionals stimulated in part by the Chartered Institute of Housing, which has played a more active role in good practice and innovation during the last five years. In addition the approach to training has shifted away from part time day release courses to a greater emphasis towards full time courses at graduate level.

In 1980 there were only three full time housing degree courses. By 1990 a wide range of graduate, post-graduate and masters' courses were on offer to complement the day-release training which had previously been the mainstay of professional housing training. This change in emphasis has injected a new, more innovative and more adaptable group into local authorities and associations, who view housing as a career rather than a job, and acknowledge customers as individuals rather than numbers on a rent roll.

The Institute's work should not be underplayed and its contribution through training and publications has assisted this process. The publication of service standards and good practice on CCT have fostered a commonly accepted non-political approach, which the Department of the Environment research papers have not always succeeded in achieving.

The third factor has been employees. The increase in educational standards, combined with a fall in potential employees of working age has encouraged employers to treat their employees as the scarce and costly commodity which they are. This has meant investing more heavily in training, from induction to exit interviews. Improvements in informing and consulting employees with an increasing use of team briefings and newsletters to ensure employees are kept informed, quality circles, multi-level working groups and suggestion schemes acknowledging employees doing the job, often have a greater understanding of the improvements which can be made. In many authorities these have developed into employee care strategies, linked but separate from enhancements to external customers (Passmore 1990). Retraining and recruiting quality staff has been a key part of enabling and fostering the change process, with a vision which is vague but is customer oriented and innovative to the environment which the organisation is facing.

Summary

- There is a strong need for change resulting from pressure in social housing. These pressures arise from a range of sources; Tenant's Choice, Citizen's Charter, CCT, competitive HAG and HIP bids and internal political pressures.

CHAPTER 3:
THE POTENTIAL FOR CHANGE

Introduction

This chapter aims to:

- offer a framework to guide the change manager in implementing a strategic change

- explain the links between customer service initiatives and its strategic implementation through mission, objectives and structured implementation programme.

Change Strategies

We have suggested so far that to adopt a fixed view of customer services is of little benefit in a highly dynamic environment. Housing organisations need to work at change to create cultures which are able to respond positively to changing customer demands and in addition which fit their external environment.

This process of constant change, however, needs to be based on a clear vision managed to achieve the desired outcome. A number of frameworks are available to assist those leading change to manage the process in a logical sequence. The two examples given, involve active participation as we believe this brings considerable benefits to employers in developing skills and to the organisation in using its employees to their full potential.

Systems Intervention Strategy

The first of these strategies consists of three overlapping phases. A diagnosis phase, in which the manager seeks to describe the problem and objectives for the change. A design phase, with alternative options developed, selected and modelled. Thirdly, the implementation phase, with its own planning and action cycles.

The strategy is a cyclical one which encourages a review of the process, before again embarking on a second cycle of change based on current perceived problems. The strategy has been applied to housing management CCT as an aid to practical application.

Phases	Steps	Actions
Diagnosis	1. Entry	* recognise change is complex
	2. Describe	* get details on CCT legislation and regulation * talk to good practice and pilot authorities * gather details on current cost and service quality * talk to tenants' groups/stakeholders informally * develop point of view on change
	3. Identify	* set outcome objectives ie. local, quality housing service
	4. Clarify	* decide on way of measures of measuring success ie. detailed and specific performance measures
Design	5. Generate	* develop ideas for a range of options for change * look at wide range of possibilities ie. LSVT, Management Buy Out, Direct Service Organisation local housing company * review objectives which may provide new options
	6. Model	* describe in detail preferred 3 options * consult tenants formally * consider for and against of each Implementation
	7. Evaluate	* test options against options agreed criteria * consider responses/views of stakeholders
	8. Design	* select preferred implementation option strategies * plan implementation
Implementation	9. Carry through	* bring together people and resources * manage process * monitor progress against timetable

While creating a more complex process to manage, in a key strategic issue such as housing management CCT, it is valuable to involve staff at all levels and other stakeholders. The initial entry step encourages those involved to discuss the general nature of change and the possible effects on staff, tenants and members.

Further by involving the team in data collection and problem description, a more detailed analysis can be obtained than would be produced if the task was carried out by senior managers.

Great thought should be given to the area of measures of success. Unless these are clearly defined, the data is available and the target is realistic the process of considering appropriate measures is wasted.

The review of options is best carried out in two stages. Firstly a wide ranging review of all possible options, from which detailed option analysis can be carried out on a select number of favoured options. The involvement of stakeholders in the evaluation process enables new perspectives to be added, before a chosen option emerges and the plan for implementation is put together.

Organisational Development Strategy

Organisational development (OD) encompasses a range of change approaches which have four common characteristics:

(i)   a planned strategy is required if change is to be managed successfully, and if the predetermined strategy is to remain appropriate to the external environment when the process has been completed.

(ii)   a range of techniques can be employed to craft the change

(iii)   the process of change is as important as the outcome

(iv)   a change manager is required to initiate the change and assist those within the organisation to successfully manage the change.

It is suggested OD is a particularly appropriate tool where an organisation is failing to achieve its objectives and the current organisation is contributing to this failure through inappropriate management styles or structure. Secondly, it can assist an organisation to develop the necessary skills to learn to manage the change. Thirdly, it can assist in implementing **new ways of** working, and for this reason it has been used widely by organisations **as a** tool in cultural change programmes.

The benefits of applying this planned approach to change may appear questionable in social housing. But in a rapidly changing environment, where for example a successful private housing tenderer who has taken over existing staff wishes to implement new working arrangements. The potential benefits may be realised.

Change is a difficult process to successfully manage, but becomes even more difficult in a changing environment. Most managers however believe they achieve change successfully. In most cases either nothing really changed, some change took place but was limited in comparison to the objectives, or the negative consequences of the process outweighed any positive gain.

Organisational development aims to minimise these potential pitfalls by creating an iterative process, and by encouraging active participation. The model has 8 steps.

Step	Action
1. Confront Environment	* survey of customers * gather information on external environment
2. Identify	* consider implications of change
3. Educate	* gather information on successful change programmes * identify good practice and innovation in housing * consider weaknesses of these approaches
4. Involvement	* encourage active participation * form working groups/customer focus groups
5. Identify Targets for Change	* establish clear objectives * plan timetable * allocate resources – staff and finance
6. Change activity	* carry out plan using timetable * monitor progress
7. Evaluate	* evaluate programme against objectives * consider impact of wider implication
8. Confront Environment	* reiterate process following changes to external environment

OD may be employed at a number of different levels and as a result the time horizons over which the cycle is repeated will change.

At the individual level, the change technique has a role to play as a counselling/development tool, it may be used to aid students in completing the Test of Professional Practice. At group and intergroup levels the technique can be employed as a team building or negotiation tool. However, it works best at the organisation-wide level. Here it can stimulate change in structures, strategy and culture. This makes it ideal, for example, for managing the changes resulting from a large scale voluntary transfer, as the fledgling organisation is forced to review working practices and operate in a new environment.

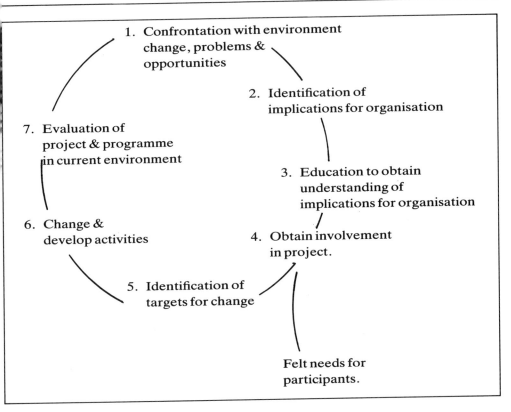

1. Confrontation with environment change, problems & opportunities

2. Identification of implications for organisation

3. Education to obtain understanding of implications for organisation

4. Obtain involvement in project.

5. Identification of targets for change

6. Change & develop activities

7. Evaluation of project & programme in current environment

Felt needs for participants.

Organisational Development Process

Reproduced with permission of OU. The Open University, P679.

Managing Change

Despite the availability of change strategies to which customer service programmes may be applied, it has been suggested (Pugh 1987) that greater planning needs to be undertaken if the process is to be successful. A planned approach will be of assistance in anticipating the need for change, correctly diagnosing the change required and managing the change process including dealing with resistance.

Four principles are of value in understanding organisational change:

* Organisations are organisms, which interact and are not logical or consistent in response to pressure. Sufficient time must be allowed for organisations to digest proposals.

* Organisations are also political systems, where change is considered not

only in terms of what's best for the organisation but what is best for people and groups. Political power will heavily influence the outcome, more than the rationality of the argument.

* All members operate as individuals, groups and organisation members and may use arguments to support their position from any one of these three standpoints.

* Those who are most successful and effective are most likely to welcome change, while those who are less successful as well as those who stand to lose from the change, will resist it.

Having considered these basic principles, six guidelines may help in managing the change process.

* The change manager must first establish the need for change. This may seem unnecessary to the change proposer, but is vital in the process of winning support and minimising resistance. This may be through explaining customer feedback from survey results, for instance, where tenants want to know in advance when the contractor will be calling.

* The second step is to think through the change, consider the costs and benefits to others involved. Will the new repairs appointment system change job content? Will it disrupt established working methods? Will it reduce autonomy? Is it to be established without consultation with staff or contractors? Once these questions have been considered the change manager is in a stronger position to understand and deal with resistance.

* Rather than presenting a full idea, it can be of advantage to initiate change through informal discussions and build on feedback to the final proposals. Participation allows commitment to grow, and for staff to think through the options. Involving staff in designing the questionnaire, analysing the results and preparing the organisations response.

* Fourthly, encourage objectives and reflect these in the proposal. By rejecting proposals the effect can be to create rigidity amongst participants. It may be necessary to phase the introduction, through a pilot scheme.

* Possibly the most difficult skill to display is a willingness by the change manager to change. If the repairs appointment system is developed by staff, it is less likely the change manager will be solely committed to the idea, and instead can remain flexible to evaluate the proposal in the light of new information.

* Finally the manager must monitor the change and seek to reinforce the

change; if the change has not settled down, review its operation and tackle the outstanding problems. If it works well the pilot project can be extended, if it needs adjustment, this can be taken on board.

Alternative Approaches

While stressing the value of a participative approach, which allows the final proposal to emerge out of discussion as a modified and reshaped plan, two alternative approaches have been suggested (Richards 1985).

A mission-orientated approach may be adopted. The change manager has a specific outcome fixed or in mind, or has been provided with a detailed brief. This may be to win a repairs contract. The assumption is that to achieve this specific end, the problem can be broken down into component parts and worked on individually. Once each job problem is solved, the component parts can be fitted together and the solution has been achieved.

While for some change problems, those of a technical nature, this approach may work, in the example a tender. However, the factors involved are imprecise and external factors outside of the change manager's control may affect the outcome.

A second option is a negotiated approach. The assumption here is that an apparently straight-forward solution can be improved by additional information which has been made available. The change manager adopts the new information, and with its supplier agrees a revised outcome. While a step towards participation, the change manager is encouraged to be highly selective about the changes adopted, rather than valuing the process of change as improvement to the result and building alliances with participants.

These alternative approaches, however, do suit situations where change is demanded at a fast pace. A need to follow a court decision overturning policy on the way the Council deals with homeless families, might benefit from a negotiated rather than full participative approach.

Understanding Resistance

Resistance is a typical response to calls for change. As a result few organisational change efforts are entirely successful. The scope of success relies more on the way the process, particularly resistance, is managed, than the soundness of the idea or its potential benefit to the organisation or its customers. The case study below looks at resistance, and how the change process can be managed to achieve a successful outcome. Because resistance arises in many different ways in individuals and groups, an assessment of the reasons is not always simple.

Resistance may arise for four basic reasons (Kotter and Schlesinger, 1979); self interest, misunderstanding, different views and low level of ability to change.

* Self interest is a very powerful factor. People involved in change proposals will ask how they are affected by them. If the effect is a negative one, the individual is likely to work to undermine the proposal, either directly, or indirectly, or fail to appreciate the wider gains available from the change.

* Misunderstanding results from a failure to explain the change proposals fully. It is a common failing to assume that as we understand the reasons for the change so does everyone else. Managers need to bring these misunderstandings to the surface quickly, and clarify the position.

* A variation of this, is that individuals may make a different assessment of a situation. Results from a tenant survey reveal that few tenants know the name of their housing officer. One reason could be that tenants forget this information, as on average the contact with the housing office is twice a year. A second reason could be the housing office fails to provide this information clearly. Each would require a different approach, the first greater contact, the second housing officer telling customers their name.

* Finally, there are in all organisations a group of individuals who have a limited ability to cope with change. They may have low self esteem and feel they will be unable to develop the new skills required, or they believe a change would be an admission of failure over the past ten years of doing the job.

There are probably an endless number of reasons why people resist change (Duncan 1977). The skilful change manager must be able to identify resistance and deal with it, to minimise its effect and where possible learn and adopt the proposals in the light of valid criticism.

Overcoming Resistance

A range of strategies are available to the change manager to help overcome resistance. There is a tendency for managers to use the style which they are comfortable with in all situations. However, one strategy may be more appropriate to one situation than another. The six options indicated (Kotter and Schlesinger) range along a continuum, from ones more appropriate to situations requiring rapid action to others at the opposite end which call for a slower speed, a less clear plan and involvement of many people to minimise resistance.

* At one extreme is participation and involvement. With the growth in tenant participation over recent years, housing professionals are likely to feel more comfortable with the process of involving potential resistors in design and implementation. The outcome of this process, as with tenant participation, is a likelihood of commitment to the proposal. However,

the change manager must be willing to see the original idea adopted and reshaped as a result of the influence of participants. The process can also become time consuming and where deadlines are present, this can make this approach of limited value.

* A second step along the road is education and communication. This will assist in minimising misunderstandings and different assessments, assuming there is a relationship of trust between those leading the change and those participating/observing the change. If there is no trust, the observers may not believe the information they are being given.

* Support and facilitation can be valuable aids when fear and anxiety lie at the heart of resistance. By providing information, training in new skills and listening, employees can be allowed to develop the confidence to cope with the change required. This approach, however, can be time consuming and expensive.

* A fourth option is negotiation; to agree the changes will take place, by trading incentives for change. This may be particularly appropriate when someone will lose out as a result of the change, and by providing other benefits they may be compensated for the loss.

* Finally, two strategies for rapid change exist; manipulation and coercion. Manipulation takes place when a manager resorts to covert attempts to influence others. This may be through the selective use of information, conscious structuring of events or co-optation of an individual or group. Co-optation differs from participation as the manager is solely seeking their endorsement rather than their ideas. The drawbacks of this approach are that employees will respond negatively to this manipulation, particularly if the manager develops a reputation for this type of approach.

Coercion too is a risky strategy, although it can allow rapid change to take place. It may leave individuals feeling resentful, but may, however, be the only option to force through predetermined but unpopular changes.

In reality change managers will aim to blend various approaches to achieve a successful outcome. They will appreciate different approaches are required with different people in different situations. The skill of managing change is selecting the right tool at the right time.

CASE STUDIES:

Welwyn Hatfield Council

The approach to customer services at Welwyn Hatfield was focused on managing change, as much as it was on specific customer care initiatives, and drew heavily on the concepts set out in this chapter.

The Council adopted a new slogan and mission statement in 1988, following a restructure of the Council's services. The mission sought to provide a vision for employees, without being over prescriptive about how to apply these aims to individual services. In tandem with the mission statement, the Council conducted a resident survey. The aim was to provide information from which the Council could review each service area, with the questions originating from service managers.

These early stages of the change process were initiated by senior managers, however, it was recognised by Management Team that to successfully stimulate lasting change, customer contact staff needed to play an active role in the process. This group would also be able to bring their first hand experiences of the service to improve and enhance the programme of change.

Approaching the topic of generating a change process in an environment which had previously been stable, it was recognised resistance would be encountered. Employees were recognised as a vital resource in providing the service and by using them to facilitate the change at a measured pace, appropriate to each service area, it was hoped a successful outcome would be achieved. Organisational development was selected as an appropriate framework because of its heavy emphasis towards participation.

With such a hazy picture there was a clear need for considerable research before embarking on a new cycle and for the change process to become continuous, because of the constant change in the local government environment. The process in stimulating customer service could be seen as a learning exercise to manage other changes to follow.

The OD model with its phases of diagnosis, involvement, detailed diagnosis, the change activity and evaluation appeared to meet these criteria.

The starting point of the process was for initial research, following up the results of the MORI survey, and collection of data on customer culture change programmes in other organisations across the public and private sectors.

Having confronted the environment both in terms of customer perceptions and general market reaction, progress could start to be made on identifying the implications of these for the housing service. A full appreciation of the issues involved was important before embarking upon a process of employee involvement. It was recognised that some employees would be resistant to the ideas of change, whichever form it took. It was suspected that resistance was likely to be highest among those who held negative views of the organisation as an employer and those of longest standing. Further, general pressure of working in front line housing would generate resistance. In an attempt to counter this, the impact of change had to be thought through; a half-baked understanding of the need for change, its impact or its goals would be more susceptible to sabotage or delay.

While a detailed plan was needed to combat resistance, the danger of adopting a detailed plan for implementation was avoided. Employees needed to generate the ideas for change, rather than endorse them, if their commitment to a new approach was to be gained and if the process of change was to offer learning and development opportunities to those involved.

The original corporate mission divided objectives into four key themes; employees, customers, strategic management and financial management.

The following **initiatives** were pursued:

Employees

* employee care policy
* flexible working
* active pursuit of equal opportunities
* team meetings
* quality circles
* staff newsletter
* suggestion scheme

Customers

* revised leaflets
* improved reception area
* service surveys
* customer contracts
* revised plain English tenant handbook
* customer focus groups

Strategic Management

* individual targets/performance indicators
* annual service plans
* 5 year strategy for each service
* revised Housing Investment Programme bid

Financial Management

* devolved accountants
* greater information to tenants on costs
* devoting budgeting to managers

A review of this reflects the similarity of initiatives to those pursued by the good practice case studies below.

The sessions were used to encourage staff within small groups to produce a shopping list of changes.

A second series of sessions led to the action plan being adopted, and groups becoming involved in implementation. The Council's housing audio cassette for visually impaired customers was produced by a working group including a repairs clerk, a housing officer and a sheltered housing worker.

Welwyn Hatfield Customer Care Code

1. We will put our customers first

2. We will keep red tape to a minimum and reply to enquiries in a plain and informative style

3. We will try to give customers other options to consider, if we cannot help

4. We will provide efficient, value for money services

5. We will take any complaint made about our services seriously and inform customers of the outcome of any investigation.

Welwyn Hatfield Employee Care Code

1. To recognise the importance of each and every employee in providing services for the people of Welwyn Hatfield

2. To support all employees in using personal initiatives to improve service quality and customer satisfaction

3. To provide good conditions of work, employment practice, including continued determination to eliminate all forms of discrimination and encourage promotion and reward within the Council, based on merit and ability

4. To continually improve effective communication at all levels, with the aim of developing better understanding and employee involvement throughout the organisation

5. To create an organisation of innovation, sound management and good practice and which is perceived to be the training ground of excellence.

Measures to determine whether the change programme was a success are difficult to identify, and are unreliable. While the initiatives were successfully implemented, staff and customer attitudes are the real test.

Tracking of staff views within the housing department revealed a growth in satisfaction and commitment to the principles of customer service. Small scale surveys of tenants, relating to individual service areas, such as repairs, also showed an improvement in service delivery.

Organisation Objectives

We have acknowledged that in most organisations customer service is viewed as a bolt-on extra, a short campaign or only relevant to staff who deal directly with the public. Customer service, however, is a means rather than an end. It is a mechanism to enable organisations to more easily and effectively achieve their own objectives.

As a strategic element it is one part of an overall plan to bring about long term change or to respond to environmental change, such as that brought about by CCT. To successfully manage this process, managers must have a clear idea of what they want to achieve and the ends by which they will achieve it. This mission, or vision, may itself be underpinned by values or codes which the organisation aims to follow. This strategy is the route map for the journey.

The mission from vision to the levels of strategy and planning forms an integrated hierarchy. Daily programmes of action link together to achieve monthly and annual plans. Each plan itself forms part of the strategy towards corporate objectives, which themselves assist the organisation to both respond to environmental pressures and move forward towards achieving the organisation's purpose. This hierarchy of programmes, strategy, objectives and purpose can be formed in most organisations.

Blackburn D.C.

Blackburn has based its organisation plan around a broad organisational cultural change programme. The starting point is a vision of what the customer wishes to achieve. By working with staff, tenants and members, a series of goals has been established which are fed into the department's five year development plan. The plan itself sets out strategic goals, bringing together private and public housing and minimising the instinctive barriers which exist between housing, planning and environmental health professionals. These are combined into annual service plans addressing customer priorities identified by surveys, monitoring feedback from tenant groups and customer forums.

Housing Objectives

* to provide an overview of the borough's housing problems and options for their solution to the members of the Council

* to utilise the Council's resources, power and influence to improve provision and standards

* wherever possible to comment, liaise with and involve local communities

---

* to identify housing need and ensure the equitable provision of services to ethnic minorities, women, disabled people, elderly people and other specific groups

* to provide an efficient, effective and caring service which places as its top priority customer care and courtesy

* to represent the views of the Council to the Association of District Councils, Members of Parliament, government departments, other agencies and to the public at large, to try to influence the development of housing policy and to attract resources into the borough

* to play a leading part in the development of anti-poverty strategies within the borough

* to provide a quality housing and welfare benefit advice service

* to work withh other departments of the Council, other agencies and voluntary organisations in the borough to assist with the development of these objectives.

Mission

The term 'mission' triggers thoughts of Captain Kirk and the Star Trek crew, whose 5 year mission was 'to boldly go where no man had gone before'.

In recent years public and voluntary sector organisations, from charities to local authorities, have begun to adopt mission statements: in the private sector these have been common practice. Arguably public sector organisations need a clearer sense of mission than private sector bodies. For the private sector the primary objective is to gain a satisfactory return on capital employed which can be disbursed as profit to shareholders. In the public and voluntary sectors a clear sense of purpose is needed if actions are to have any meaning. These organisations in their missions must be seen to be making a positive contribution to society. A problem which faces those setting a mission is internal conflict. For associations, particularly charitable associations, the purpose may be clearer. For local authorities the vague aims of improving or sustaining the quality of life in their district are likely to result in conflicts between different priorities; new housing versus leisure facilities, economic development versus planning control.

For both sorts of organisation a second issue is that of differentiating ends from means if the mission is vague and abstract. We have already accepted that in a hierarchy of objectives, one person's means may be another person's ends. So an objective for the Public Relations Unit may be to produce a new tenants' handbook. For the Council these may be seen at a corporate level as a means of using an effective medium to explain the Council's message about cuts in housing services or about the service standards customers may expect. However, at any one level of the organisation's hierarchy, ends should be consistent between teams or departments.

A third issue is the rapidly changing environment which social housing organisations find around them. The response may be to ignore a public statement of mission, to keep such a statement vague or to ignore the published mission as circumstances dictate. This divergence between official goals and operational goals is common. Operational goals are themselves more likely to reflect individual or power group interests. An association's official mission may be to tackle homelessness. However, as a result of funding for shared ownership, it may instead target effort towards shared ownership development, not because this makes a contribution towards those most in need but because it keeps the development team employed and assists the growth of the association. The operational mission may be more subtle than this. It may have more to do with personal gain than benefits which will accrue to the organisation.

A mechanism to deal with divergence and conflict is to have a specific primary mission supplemented by a secondary mission and values.

Orbit Housing Association

Orbit is the 15th largest association in the country and is now on its second medium term strategic plan, which formalises objectives for the coming three years in addition to reviewing mission and values.

Having gained experience from its 1989–1992 plan, the second plan is well developed and explicit about Orbit's aims.

Orbit's mission is to:

"Maximise the provision of affordable homes and manage its stock to the highest standards".

The mission statement offers a primary objective, 'provision of affordable housing' and a secondary objective, management standards. The Orbit plan, however, differs from the many other business plans which form the basis of publicity and information for funders; the Orbit plan sets out how it is seeking to achieve these aims. The six value statements provide a guide to managers and influence the subsequent strategic plans contained later in the document under the headings development, housing management, finance, people and performance indicators.

Value Statements:

* developing the maximum number of multi-tenure, well designed homes within the financial reach of those in greatest need

* provide a professional, efficient and understanding housing management service, which reflects its customers' needs

* maintain the stock through a cost effective carefully planned and responsive maintenance service

* planning its ongoing financial security through prudent risk management, to ensure ultimate accountability

* promote equality of opportunity across all activities and offering a positive working environment

* participating in national housing debate and promoting its innovative, wide ranging and caring services.

Organisational values and strategic planning

Organisation values seek to offer guidance to those considering mechanisms and strategies to fulfil the organisation mission. These values are a code of conduct, like a walker following the country code or a professional their professional body's conduct code.

A number of additional constraints face voluntary and local authorities in strategic planning. These result from the fact that social housing bodies operate in a complex environment in which many stakeholders seek to influence and control operations, and both local authorities and associations rely on other bodies to complete their tasks. In the case of local authorities this may include voluntary bodies who are increasingly becoming providers, leaving local councils to co-ordinate provision.

Social housing does face some difficulties, in measuring an intangible service, which seeks to deliver goods to many customers. These may range from government bodies, to homeless families. If multiple goals are pursued, as we suggest, these may conflict.

The problem grows as the power of stakeholders is not equal. Without pressure from the Housing Corporation homeless families can be quickly forgotten by associations. Evidence suggests that despite the priorities of local authorities, housing association performance in this area is less than positive (Roof 1993).

Families remain in bed and breakfast while some associations continue giving priority to transfers and estate rehousing for the sons and daughters of existing tenants, and to applicants from their own lists who may already be adequately housed.

Employees may work to undermine predetermined strategies. This may be explicit because of professional bias towards certain codes of conduct or because it enhances the standing of their department or their personal progression. More difficult to identify and to deal with is covert action to undermine corporate strategy. The internal politics of large organisations frequently result in covert departmental battles for resources and power, even after priorities have been decided.

External agencies, be it the Department of the Environment, District Auditor or Housing Corporation are also likely to take a keen interest in internal management. For associations, the Housing Corporation's power extends to replacing board members and appointing staff to take management action to resolve management problems.

The effect of multiple stakeholders, professional prejudices and external monitors, is to restrain rewards and sanctions. This, in itself, limits management innovation, and encourages reactive management, with the formal publication of goals seen as wasted effort.

Shelter

Shelter is one of Britain's largest charities employing almost 200 staff scattered across the country in housing aid centres, in addition to its core of policy and campaign workers based in London.

In the late 1980s the charity executive recognised a need to review Shelter's forward planning process and employed consultants to develop a three year planning model to assist Shelter take forward its role in the 1990s. As an organisation which relies heavily on the commitment of its staff, and with a tendency to attract articulate individuals the organisation has had a history of collective management. The consultants recognized the importance of this in developing a management tool to enable the management team and executive to steer the organisation, while not removing the benefits of staff commitment.

Following discussions with staff and a review of the organisation, the consultants made the following proposals:

* the development of an agreed 'vision and values' statement was fundamental to Shelter's work

* aims needed to be developed for the organisation; 'development aims' relating to external work and 'maintenance aims' concerned with reviewing the internal operation of the organisation

* the introduction of management system; planning and supervision

* planning goals should be realistic and use the minimum of paper.

The starting point was to agree a vision statement. With multiple interest groups and strong commitment from staff, board members and management team, the process was more difficult than for developing a statement for a small local authority housing department with twenty staff.

Initial groups were formed to talk about the vision statement, each contained a mix of staff, senior managers and executive board members. The views of the groups were fed together and with facilitation from the consultants a final draft was produced.

Further work was carried out to review future plans and again consultants assisted in this process. Annual plans were produced for each of the four divisions, which are reviewed annually and linked to the budget development process, so resources can be targeted towards planning priorities.

The flexibility of the system works well. Further enhancement has taken place in 1993, in an attempt to produce a series of three year organisation objectives. These form part of the divisional plans which individually must seek to implement action during the year to move the organisation closer to its three year organisation goal.

In its 1993/94 plan Objective 2 was 'to eliminate the abuse of temporary housing'. This is translated to an annual aim for 1993/94 to eliminate the use of bed and breakfast. To achieve this the four divisions each identified actions relating to B & B. The campaign division identified the need to run a campaign around B & B, focusing towards good practice and economic arguments. The information for the campaign is the responsibility of the Housing Services division, who aim to identify good and bad practice authorities, lobby specific authorities and identify alternative forms of temporary accommodation. Shelter Scotland too will pick up the campaign and examine Scottish examples of bad practice, lobbying these authorities.

The integration aims to ensure resources are better targeted, and more importantly that Shelter is producing a single focused message. The success of Shelter's focused management approach can be measured by the charity's success. Its success in safeguarding the rights of homeless people during a period of deregulation and for advancing the arguments of improved targeting of resources.

Summary

- To produce a customer service culture managers need to craft change using the skills and knowledge of all employees in the organisation. Two techniques are available which offer high levels of participation; system intervention strategy and organisational development.

- Customer service needs to form part of a clear strategy of managing change, based on a vision of the organisation's employees. The use of this approach has been applied by a number of bodies across the statutory and voluntary sectors.

CHAPTER 4:
MANAGEMENT OBJECTIVES

Introduction

This chapter aims to:

- explain previous management approaches to generating advantage in a competitive environment

- analyse the current interest in excellence, culture and change management

- reveal the wide spread application of these approaches beyond the social housing environment

- identify common themes of customer service and people management

Scientific Management

The roots of bureaucracy lie in scientific management which aimed to remove indivudual discretion and standardise processes and outputs.

Bureaucracy has become a term of criticism, but offers efficiency through standardisation. Max Weber's (1947) codification brought academic credibility to a management approach based on written rules and established procedures, where tasks were divided between specialists and progress was on the basis of merit rather than birth.

As users of most public services have learnt, the strengths of bureaucracy can quickly be hidden by the rigidity of behaviour where 'it's more than my job's worth' mentality brings frustration for customers and results in defensive employees. Departmentalism adds to these problems for customers as specialists limit their roles to artificially created barriers. Whether it's Watford or Walsall, the problems can be almost insurmountable, as a Walsall Area Housing Manager explained:

"At times, I felt it was like the middle ages, you know, Black Death was going to be the next thing. But I underestimated the bureaucracy. I rang the environmental health department. 'There's rats in Goscote. Could you give us some advice?' 'Oh, you speak to public works'. So I ring public works. 'Where are the rats?' 'Goscote'. 'No, are they above or below ground? If they are below ground, they are our responsibility, if they are above, you'll have to ring the environmental health department'. 'You're kidding me'. 'No', they said, 'that's the way it works'." Seabrook (1984)

Much of local government has failed to break away from strict departmentalism based on specialist and professional attitudes.

Structure

A second area which has attracted attention is organisational structure. It is through organisation structure that grand design is translated into operational reality. This fascination with structure has dominated organisation development for decades. Employees now expect a new boss to bring a new organisation structure.

Little, however, is made of the importance of 'fit' between internal resources and an organisation's competitive environment, or of organisation models which may provide a greater understanding of organisation dynamics. In practice this may explain why so many reorganisations fail to deliver the gains envisaged at the design stage of greater efficiency or improved service delivery.

A detailed model of organisation structure has been developed (Mintzberg 1979), which describes six model organisation types; simple structure, machine bureaucracy, professional bureaucracy, multi-divisional, adhocracy and missionary. Each model type relies on a co-ordinating mechanism. This mechanism aims to ensure management control. If an inappropriate structure is selected by managers this can prove fatal. A highly participative, collective decision making structure would be inappropriate in a large organisation, which was operating in a rapidly changing environment. A thousand strong DLO could not effectively discuss and collectively agree a tender price for housing repairs, while a two person family owned plumbing business could.

Job Enrichment

The over concern for bureaucracy, and attention towards hierarchical structure and procedures, brought rigidity and low levels of employee commitment. Efforts to overcome these inherent problems focused on team approach and employee motivation.

Herzberg (1966) suggested that two factors influenced job satisfaction; hygiene factors contributed to job dissatisfaction, while motivators led to job satisfaction. Hygiene factors were claimed to relate to people's basic needs and included working conditions and pay. Motivators related more to the need to experience psychological growth and included achievement, recognition, responsibility and enhancement.

These moves towards team working have been most successful in manufacturing and were most notably adopted in Japan, but also brought benefits to European producers like Rover Cars, who have adopted the approach in the 1990s.

Whilst the approach has had a major impact on manufacturing, its impact to date on public services in particular and office work in general has been minimal. This is increasingly likely to change as housing organisations attempt to break away from the bureaucratic structure of multi-layer organisations and replace these with short reporting structures which rely on team participation for monitoring performance and sharing experiences.

Whether the service sector will be able to push beyond this to the post Fordism models being trailed in manufacturing is questionable, although the efforts of local government reorganisation such as Tower Hamlets' Neighbourhood Town Hall and Islington's neighbourhood approach, with a number of services sharing a building and more generic working, may be the start of this move away from specialisation. The complexity of legislation and standards limits the ability to achieve full integration at the professional level. While, reception and support staff have common roles, generic care officers are limited in their ability to deal competently with all the issues facing their clients from health and social work to housing.

Culture

What do we mean by culture? The term has become a standard phrase in management, but definitions differ widely. Tom Peters (1982) has defined it as 'the way we do things around here', others consider it to be shared customs and traditions. Another view suggests organisations do not have a single culture, but share a number of sub-cultures, each dominating in different areas within the organisation.

The upsurge in interest in culture has brought a new approach which sees culture as an element within all organisations, but which is variable. It can be moulded and changed by management through a process of top down cultivation. It is this feature which has brought it to the attention of management in the belief that if organisations can get their culture 'right' all else will fall into place.

A second viewpoint is of culture as an outcome of processes and events, which bring a shared meaning and understanding to employees about their organisation. In this latter case the process of managing cultural change is less certain and involves recognising patterns of events rather than creating a vision to be installed throughout the organisation.

It is this second definition which we advocate as a model for change in a world which is complex, dynamic and chaotic. This approach requires a more considered approach to change, crafting a strategy requiring dedication, experience, mastery of detail, and integration.

While different to the quick fix of the US management gurus which we look at, this more dynamic approach fits in to the chaotic world of housing that does not demand one solution of simple customer orientation, but a myriad of solutions. At the centre may be a customer focus, but it must encompass an array of other approaches which are constantly changing.

Before moving on to consider the work of Peters and post modernism, it is worth briefly considering a range of cultural models which exist. These models provide a useful framework to evaluate organisations at first glance.

Cultural Types

The classic cultural model suggests four cultural types (Handy 1976). These are power, role, task and person cultures. While these are presented as distinct models, in practice the boundaries between each are blurred.

The power culture is dependent on a strong central power source, from whom power radiates through hand picked senior staff who think and act in an approved way. As a result the organisation needs few rules or procedures, and can react quickly to new challenges and threats. Their ability to react in the right way or respond to the real rather than imaginary dangers depends on the person at the centre. This person can make or break the organisation with a few key decisions.

Robert Maxwell was an archetypical power culture leader. All key decisions were taken by him and his key advisers. No one knew the full picture of his operations which reduced the influence of his subordinates.

The culture attracts individuals who are power-orientated and who are risk takers. The major risk comes when the power source leaves or dies; this vacuum can destroy the organisation. Few examples of this exist in the public sector, although some housing associations are dominated by a single Chief Executive, but public accountability through the Housing Corporation reduces the opportunity for total dominance.

The role culture is based on the traditional bureaucracy. Decision making is based on logic and reason. Tasks are divided into specialisms and functions with clearly established procedures. This culture attracts employees who wish to minimise risk and seek security or conformity. It is typically found in state organisations which experience little change, allowing procedures to become established beyond their simple values as a tool to achieve the required outputs. Local government, as well as banking and the civil service, display this culture.

The recent injection of competition into local government has brought change.

Pressure is now on to create result-orientated cultures. Similar pressures are at work in housing associations, who must compete for finance from the Housing Corporation, as well as presenting a business-orientated approach to funders.

The task culture is job or project-orientated. The outcome is of sole consideration, as opposed to the process. As a result the culture fits well in a dynamic and chaotic environment where constant change is required. The task culture may offer solutions to the bureaucratic traditions of local government. Its problem is maintaining control, as structures are flat and team based. The recent injection of competition into the public sector demands attention to both process and outcome: Was the house let on the basis of housing need to the applicant with the highest number of points, as well as, was it let quickly? This presents a contradicition, as neither objective can be fully satisfied. A balancing act is sought between process and outcome.

The final 'person' culture is restricted to small organisations. It may fit a housing co-op or tenants' federation. This culture comes about as a result of a group of individuals deciding to group together for mutual benefit. Such groups need to be small, and are only manageable through mutual consent. When this breaks down, the group either fails to operate effectively or falls apart.

Excellence Organisations

The recent emphasis on culture has been inspired by American management writers, particularly Peters and Waterman, but also Kanter, Deal and Kennedy. All have suggested that culture plays a major part in the success of excellent organisations.

The most successful of these publications has been by Peters and Waterman, who identified a need in America for a recipe for success. The early work of the authors suggested a simplistic formula, which they claimed to have identified from a study of US private sector companies. The formula is based on a popular culture of keeping things simple, and breaking away from the classic business school techniques of cost curves, business matrices and econometric models. They suggested eight criteria, that if applied would bring organisation excellence.

Eight criteria of Organisational Excellence

* 'Managing ambiguity and paradox' – a recognition that organisations may pursue apparently conflicting aims.

* 'A bias for action' – a preference for getting on with the job rather than engaging in excessive analysis, a feature of bureaucratic organisations.

> * 'Close to the Customer' – a wish to show interest and concern for customer needs by listening and talking to customers about the product.
>
> * 'Autonomy' – involves leaving individuals and teams to do the job they do best without excessive supervision.
>
> * 'Productivity through People' – here employees are acknowledged as the key resource, without whom the organisation cannot be a success.
>
> * 'Stick to the Writing' – re-emphasises the importance of concentrating on what the company knows best.
>
> * 'Simple form – less staff' – through which a small team of senior people can co-ordinate organisation activities.
>
> * 'Simultaneous loose-tight properties' – involve control through values while giving employees the scope to be entrepreneurial.

When combined Peters and Waterman suggest these rules create an environment where employees are motivated to excell and where outcomes are perceived by individuals as personal success.

This wish to create large organisations which were responsive to their external environment was a theme echoed by Kanter (1985) who in less overt terms argued that large organisations should empower their employees to take decisions.

Critics have not been slow to identify weaknesses in the early 1980s management approach, although much of the criticism was the way in which the books, particularly 'In Search of Excellence', pandered to managerial rather than academic readers. The style was chatty and the approach to case studies informal.

More substantive criticisms have been made by academics. They have argued that the methodology used was at best questionable. Peters and Waterman make no reference in the publication to the scale of the study or information on the data collected and analysed (Guest 1992). Of greater concern, and acknowledged later by Peters, was the failure to consider the external environment. It was assumed excellence was sufficient in itself. External factors and implementation problems would be overcome by applying the 8 basic criteria. The failure of some of the 'excellence' companies quoted by Peters revealed this weakness. His second book 'A Passion for Excellence', written jointly with Nancy Austin, focused more sharply on leadership and innovation. It was not until Peters' third publication that the importance of the external environment was acknowledged in full. 'Thriving on Chaos' picks up the role of the leader, but rather than offering a prescriptive solution suggests a need for managers to constantly review their external environment and their corporate strategy, with the objective of constant adaption of strategy to fit environmental pressures. The most recent publication continues this theme (Peters 1992).

Change Organisations

With an increasingly dynamic environment the final step in the cultural minefield has been the recognition of chaos.

Previously, management theories suggested the world could be modelled and outcomes of events predicted: that applying one approach brought a predetermined outcome. Reality tells us this is untrue. The world is unpredictable, irrational and chaotic.

With its roots in post modernist theory, chaos management theory acknowledges the messy disorganisation surrounding firms which are in a constant state of change. Rather than attempt to create order, Peters and Handy now suggest managers need to learn to manage in this chaotic environment. This may be through a structural approach. The Shamrock organisation (Handy 1989) breaks the mould of traditional employment patterns, where all workers are contracted employees. The Shamrock organisation divides workers, providing greater flexibility by mixing core workers with contractors and flexible workforce. While core workers receive all the benefits of permanent employment; sick pay,

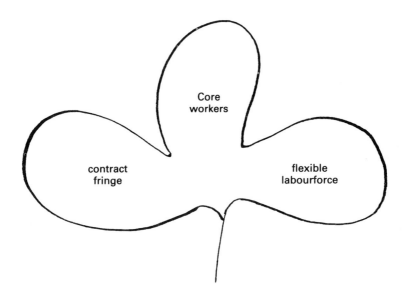

pensions and other employee benefits, contractors and peripheral workers are employed on short fixed term contracts which offer few of these benefits. This approach can already be seen as associations and management organisations enter the housing CCT arena, buying in staff on fixed term contracts.

Alternatively, rather than adopting a strong corporate culture, an organisation may adopt weaker cultures, which are more adaptable to change, or distinctive cultures which fit different aspects of their business. A local authority may hold within its corporate culture a series of sub-cultures; a business-focused culture within the DSO, a political-citizenship culture within the democracy unit and a customer-focused culture within client departments.

In the price competitive world of housing CCT it may be assumed the local authorities who have focused attention on customer service cultures in response to 'Tenants Choice' will be automatically ahead of the field. The answer is obviously no. While customer service provides a potential for differentiation and a route to achieving a quality threshold, a disregard for the contractual terms and pricing will leave the customer service organisation out in the cold. To be most effective the contractor must operate to the agreed quality standards which customers have requested based on surveys and which are included in the specifications. In a well managed operation the internal contractor will already be operating to this standard and so will be placed in a strong position to tender successfully on price and quality.

Lessons from Britain and the United States

The following pages of this chapter review good practice examples from the British and US public and private sectors. Traditionally housing managers have argued that customer services is of limited value. These examples reveal the wide spread use of customer services as a management tool.

US Public Housing

'On Monday 12 December 1988 a nine year old boy had an asthma attack at home in the Dearborn Homes project on the south side of Chicago. The ambulance which came in response to a telephone call from a neighbour was, according to one version of events, pelted with stones and eggs when it arrived. The paramedical staff drove away from the building until police appeared, then returned and climbed a darkened stairway to the fifth floor. The child had gone into respiratory attack and died later in hospital.' (Hambleton, 1990)

The US public housing experience bears some similarities to the British experience, but is different in its political, economic and legal aspects. Launched in the 1930s as part of the national recovery package, via the Public Housing Act 1937, US public housing has grown to over 1.3 million units. As a percentage of the total stock it represents a mere 3%, and houses those at the bottom of the US economy. A high proportion of tenants are black or Hispanic. However, like British public housing it is in decline.

In Britain the 1980s saw a withdrawal of resources from public housing. This situation was mirrored in the US, during the Reagan administration, despite calls for investment to tackle an aging stock in poor repair, the large numbers of vacancies, rent strikes and race problems. During the Reagan administration the budget for low income housing was slashed by 78% from $31 billion to $6.9 billion.

The public housing authorities are managed in a similar way to housing associations. A Board of Commissioners, appointed by the City Mayor, takes policy and strategy decisions and paid officials who operate in a less politically charged environment than local authority officers, conduct day to day affairs.

Disaffection with public housing authorities spread during the 1980s and a search began for alternative models for management. Five alternative models were identified as a means to improve residents' and citizens' view of public housing, while retaining collective ownership. Other options more favoured by the Reagan administration were routes to spread ownership or privatisation of estates.

Tenant participation had played a low-key role in some US public housing authorities during the 1970s. These had, in the main, arisen following tenant rent strikes or protests on estates. Generally of a formal nature, operating through Tenant Advisory Councils, they enabled tenants to get involved with selection of new tenants, dealing with tenant disputes and representation of the Board. This concept of participation is at the higher rungs of the Arnstein ladder of tenant participation, popularised by TPAS. While in Britain a substantial number of councils express a commitment to the ideals of tenant involvement, this level of participation is rare.

The second option was resident management. Supporters of resident management argue that tenants are not only capable of taking over the management functions but, when they do, indirect benefits can be gained. This is the view of Bob Rigby, Director at Jersey City Housing Authority (Rigby, 1989 and 1982).

CASE STUDIES

Jersey City Housing Authority

Jersey City Housing Authority (JCHA) has a stock of 4,000 units and houses those from the lowest socio-economic groups. Through the creation of local management boards, management standards and social indicators have improved. In management terms voids have fallen from 20% to 3%, arrears 30%

down to 6%. Social factors such as crime rates and community involvement also reflect the change in management style.

Three elements were fundamental to turning round JCHA estates;

* a working partnership with estate tenant organisations

* organisation of estate and agency management

* capital improvements

To achieve any turn round on problem estates, the commitment of community leaders was accepted as vital. Only community action can tackle drug dealing, prostitution and organised theft, and evict these elements from the estate. Such a strategy of involvement takes time and effort to create and sustain. The development of trust, the first step in any relationship, is accomplished only gradually through shared experiences and discussion. Having gained the trust of community leaders, training and assisting them to build a community organisation can be equally difficult.

The second element is the negotiation of a contract between the housing authority and the tenants. In a similar approach to Priority Estate Project, JCHA have established on site managers with local resident handypersons and repairs budgets. The local focus ensures problems get sorted quickly and vandalism is dealt with by a mixture of repair and peer pressure.

The final element is a commitment to tackle the years of neglect, by investment in the estate. In JCHA this too is a partnership between tenants and the housing authority with priorities being set by tenants and funding from JCHA.

JCHA is held up as a model in the US as to what can be achieved in public housing for the very poor through good management and involving customers in a partnership.

The third option brings together ownership and management, through a Community Development Corporation (CDC). This has a similar role to the UK Housing Action Trusts, with a focus towards area regeneration, but with greater resident involvement. Having completed improvement works CDCs frequently turn themselves into the two remaining models; a co-op or mutual association. Both models are rare, and involve a change in ownership, with legal and financial implications.

An evaluation of the alternatives identified that resident management was most likely to bring the greatest benefit to tenants. However, it was also considered a costly option in administration terms. Changes in ownership, too, were problematical and relied too heavily on a body of active tenants with a good knowledge and considerable commitment. In the US these housing factors were not often present.

The failure of public housing in the US, according to the study, lay in its failure to successfully manage a large scale bureaucracy at the small estate level. The idea that small is beautiful has previously gained popularity. It was suggested (Schumacher 1973) that five principles were important for managing large organisations, while preventing their size leading to inefficiency and remoteness.

These five principles are:

*   subsidiarity   – the importance of delegating decisions to the lowest level

*   vindication   – the need for managers to support decisions of junior staff

*   identification – the need for each unit to operate under its own balance sheet

*   motivation   – the importance of reason and challenge to be associated with work

*   middle axiom – the need to balance order and discipline, with abandon and entrepreneurship

There are similarities which can be drawn between these five principles and the eight excellence criteria. The 'middle axiom' is similar to the 'loose-tight' concept of achieving flexibility while retaining control. 'Simple form, lean staff', and 'subsidiarity' concepts too overlap, as do 'identification' and 'Autonomy and Entrepreneurship'.

British housing is generally on a larger scale than US Public Housing Authorities, managing on average 5,000 units for a local authority compared to 2,500 units in the US. While housing professionals have noticed the remoteness of centralised housing departments, and have responded through decentralisation strategies, the scale and level of decentralisation has been limited, with a few exceptions.

The housing association movement's response has been worse. The effects of scattered developments resulting from the removal of zoning, has meant tenants can be 30-60 minutes' drive from their closest housing office. With no local management, no tenant involvement and no local representatives, HA tenants can feel cut off and isolated.

The US experience suggests a positive model to improve resident satisfaction, and tackle estate management problems, through a local approach which considers the needs of individual estates rather than cities or districts from a remote office bureaucracy.

British Airways

BA offers an interesting model of change to social housing practitioners. As a loss making public sector airline BA has transformed itself into one of the few commercially successful airlines in the world, through a clear business strategy which has at its heart the customer.

A comparison between a social housing organisation and British Airways may, at first glance, appear irrelevant. They are distanced by the profit motive, as well as business operation. However, similarities are clear, both offer a product which requires a technical input, while perceived as a service industry. Both operate in a unionised and highly regulated environment, and both rely on people contact for customer perception of quality.

BA's customer initiatives have drawn most attention. The first of these was symbolic of the changes to core. New uniforms were designed for cabin staff and a new logo joined the refreshed management team. This change was accompanied by loud messages from senior management of a change in focus, away from a technical focus towards marketing and customer.

To implement this change in focus, an organisation restructure aimed to reduce bureaucracy and the size of the corporate core. Effort was made to decentralise functions and empower unit managers. The restructure created independent strategic business units, and unit managers were charged with the responsibility of becoming profitable, managing their resources, both technical and human, to generate income. Such an approach could have become fragmented but strong corporate value for market orientation drew each element together to provide a collective consciousness.

As part of the package British Airways looked to reduce the size of its work force through redundancy while building up loyalty among those that remained by increasing employee involvement through customer care teams and quality circles. These objectives appear in contradiction, as the outcome of redundancy plans is often a significant fall in morale. A voluntary approach to redundancy eased the problem. Staff involvement was complemented by an active training programme designed to both improve customer awareness of employees and focus attention on the need for all employees to contribute to competitiveness.

The third element after restructuring and retraining was performance monitoring. Having identified the business and their customers, British Airways wanted to chart their progress in winning back customers. The measures of hard data ranged across customer contact points:

B.A. Performance Monitoring

(a)   on first contact with passengers at a sales shop –

* acceptable maximum waiting time
* evidence of up-to-date sales material
* comfort of the environment

(b)   when telephoning to make a reservation –

* speed of answer
* additional facilities offered

(c)   at airport check in –

* number of counters open
* queuing times
* use of passenger's name

(d)   during the flight –

* availability of offered amenities
* speed at which calls are answered
* cleanliness

(e)   on arrival at destination –

* adequacy of announcements
* transfer arrangements
* adequacy of baggage retrieval.

The key measure, however, was profitability. For those who achieved high results, pay rewards followed.

These elements were complemented by a continuous follow-up of programmes which returned to the overriding theme of competitive edge through customer orientation. Each was based on customer survey results and the central idea was to continually repeat the message through different examples. The results have placed British Airways in a strong position to take on US International carriers for the ten or so places as a major world airline in the 21st Century.

Dangers do exist in taking the competitive strategy too far. The episode in 1992 involving Virgin Airways demonstrates the need to act both ethically and legally.

BA's success has been achieved by focusing on both the core business of carrying people safely and economically and recognising that travellers come back if well treated. In addition identifying different segments of the market offers potential opportunities. Business users want quality as well as personal perks from business travel; airmiles offered an added bonus. Parents paying the bill for lone children, want safety for their youngster during the trip. British Airways' response to this need has been the Young Flyer Service, which offers to accompany the child throughout the trip.

British Telecom

BT was privatised in 1984 in the first popular privatisation share sale. Since 1984 profitability has risen, along with customer satisfaction as the business has been transformed from GPO 1960s' management to customer focused delivery of the 1990s.

A policy of change was initiated in 1986 by BT UK, although it has subsequently been integrated into every part of the three main divisions; BT UK Communication systems and BT International as well as their subsiduaries, and affects the workforce of some 250,000 people.

The driving force behind the change came from three main areas of concern which confronted the newly privatised management team:

* competition: the removal of state control opened BT to market competition across its business
* need to reduce, as a public utility, social cost: social goals as well as business ones were pursued. While in part some social goals were retained, BT recognised the need to reduce cost if share holders were to receive a return and investment income was to be generated to improve the network.
* culture: the culture was one of a civil service bureaucracy with highly compartmentalised roles. This was inappropriate for a business entering a fast moving market place.

Quality

To tackle these issues the new approach BT adopted was based on quality. The aim was to meet customer requirements first time, every time as part of the normal business activity. Implementation relied on a restructuring of the business away from hierarchical systems to team based structures, with a high level of communication and participation, both of these being used as tools to stimulate the move from old style to new style management.

More recently the structure has changed further towards a matrix organisation at the senior level, as the three major businesses are integrated to gain synergies between business areas.

The quality projects began in 1986 with the launch of Total Quality Management (TQM), and was seen as a way of developing the new team based approach. The quality programme had two specific objectives:

*   to achieve an increase in team problem solving
*   to provide opportunities to stimulate the cultural change programme.

Multi-disciplinary teams were set up across specialisms and hierarchies to pursue quality improvement issues. The monitoring of the teams was carried out by Quality Councils using the Crosby five project approach;

*   define the problem
*   conduct problem analysis and planning
*   prepare action plans
*   develop implementation plans
*   implement.

Thus they were able to approve, set and monitor quality outputs of the teams.

Training

BT recognised the need to resource and reskill employees to both deal with technological innovation and business management and to develop the participation skills for the quality programme.

The technical/managerial training has sought to provide a constant updating, so managers stay in touch with good management principles, as well as business objectives and market changes. Accompanying this are a series of programmes to provide tools and techniques, ranging from initial awareness sessions at the start of the programme and developing into three day workshops.

Communication

Communication is seen as a vital element in the change programme. The starting point was to assist employees to understand BT's business, the changes of a competitive environment, post-privatisation and BT's mission. This was achieved through awareness sessions to which all employees were invited.

The process was continued through the development of a communications strategy within the revised organisation structure. The strategy was supported by the appointment of an Employee Communications Manager who was responsible for monitoring implementation.

Part of the strategy consisted of the introduction of team briefings. These were adopted to become a two-way flow, rather than employee briefings, although it was acknowledged that the flow of information up the hierarchy is both more limited and difficult to sustain.

Other initiatives have included staff suggestion schemes, with a particular focus toward saving money, and employee surveys and joint customer/employee working groups.

Employee response

Consultation with employees over change has reduced resistance to other initiatives in the package of changes which have sought to move the organisation away from its public sector roots. The removal of demarcation barriers to prevent duplicated calls on customers by two specialist engineers, the introduction of performance related pay and appraisals have been successfully introduced. The Trade Union response has, in general, been positive, particularly to training initiatives and employee consultation. Specific concerns were expressed about personal targets and personal pay packages, which reduced the potential for collective bargaining.

Cost

It is suggested quality saves money, and this argument is difficult to disprove, as the issue of lost customer business and inefficiency are notoriously difficult to cost accurately. BT, however, estimate the programme has cost approximately £4 million per annum, and while tangible cost savings from the suggestion scheme or other initiatives are minimal in comparison, both customer satisfaction and profits have continued to rise over the period.

Summary

- In generating change and stimulating the development of a customer service strategy, managers need to develop processes and structure to support the change programme.

- Customer service is a popular management approach at present, but other approaches have been taken; bureaucratic management, structural change and job enrichment have all been popular. Others such as excellence and cultural change remain as strands within customer service.

- In crafting change the experiences of other organisations can help guide managers. The experiences of Jersey City, BA and BT reveal the importance of listening to customer needs and valuing staff as the most valuable resource available to the organisation.

- These organisations recognised that it is their employees which are their greatest resources. By investing time, effort and money and in staff greater efficiency and quality can be achieved.

CHAPTER 5:
PUBLIC SERVICE
ORIENTATION

Introduction

This chapter aims to:

● explain the ideas behind the growth in popularity of customer service in the public sector

● identify weaknesses in the consumerist approach to customer service

● identify the principles behind the Citizens' Charter and consider its application within social housing.

The Concept of PSO

The concept of public service orientation has its roots firmly in the literature on excellence. It too identifies the need for clear leadership from managers and council members. This chapter reviews the development of public service orientation, its influence on the current debate on public service principles and its application.

Public service orientation was promoted via a series of papers published by the Local Government Training Board (Stewart and Clarke 1985 and 1986), Public Administration (Stewart and Clarke 1987) and Local Government Policy Making (Clarke and Stewart 1987(a) 1987(b)). While its core is service delivery, it advances a series of propositions which define the boundaries of the concept, and attempt to differentiate PSO from the 'excellence' concept of the American private sector. These may be summarised as:

* local authorities exist to provide service for the public;

* a local authority will be judged by the quality of service provided within the resources available;

* the service provided is only of real value if it is of value to those for whom it is provided;

* those for whom services are provided are customers demanding high quality service; and

* quality of service demands closeness to the customer.

As a result they argue that local authorities should focus attention on:

* closeness to the customer

* listening to the public

* access for the public

* seeking our views, suggestions and complaints

* the public's right to know

* quality of service

* the public as a test of quality.

This desire to provide services 'for' the public, rather than 'to' the public, is hindered in local authorities which have closed themselves off from the public. These organisations are characterised by:

* buildings that do not invite
* the unhelpful response on the telephone
* the form that is difficult to complete
* the time spent waiting
* the letter that is difficult to understand
* the lack of explanation as to why an application is refused
* the complaint that is only dealt with when raised by a Councillor.

Breaking down these artificial barriers, Stewart and Clarke (1987) argue, is a shared responsibility between management, employees and elected members. They recognise that there may be resistance to this approach from members who feel they were elected to represent the public and are in touch with issues, from management who may believe that professional judgements will allow them to determine service quality unfettered by individual prejudice, and from staff who may prefer formal and detached relationships with customers.

The hands-on approach by Clarke and Stewart (1987a) specifically identifies the barriers which organisations erect, and discusses mechanisms to begin removing these barriers to effective service delivery by drawing on the experiences of both progressive British local authorities and examples from Sweden. Steps to open up the authority include publication of consumer indicators and establishing standards for the core services.

While the theme of the citizen is written small in the early PSO articles, the theoretical debate prepared the ground for the Citizens' Charter which has moved public services from the privatisation-is-all debate of the Thatcher years to a recognition that public services should be accountable to the public and offer value for money both to users and to all stakeholders.

The PSO Debate

PSO and Citizenship

One of the early criticisms of the PSO concept (Rhodes 1987) suggests that this approach, while placing an emphasis on service delivery, needed itself to be set in a broader perspective. This has subsequently been recognised by Clarke and Stewart (1987(b)), who have broadened their focus to incorporate open government and participation.

Rhodes added to the service delivery core, which he terms 'consumerism', two further 'Cs'; caring and citizenship.

Caring is implicit within the discussions of PSO, as it acknowledges the importance of providing services for customers and argues that local authorities should respect people's wants. This can be achieved by improving the mechanism for listening to customers' views, encouraging feedback and by establishing mechanisms to enable identified wants to be met.

However, while implicit, caring should be acknowledged explicitly as an organisation's core value. If service delivery is a surface principle, it must be underpinned by a series of values which guide management behaviour in the way the service is delivered.

The third C is that of citizenship, a concept which involves both rights and responsibilities. To the Greeks it was fundamental to a person's role in society.

> "The Greek Citizen (Polites) was the man who practised politics, who participated in the affairs of the city state (Polis). Every citizen fulfilled deliberative and adjudicative functions.... The 'polis' was a conventional web of relations which was sustained by the speaking and acting together of a plurality of people. Only a god or beast could live outside the 'polis'. Man could only live and act meaningfully within it". (Van Gunsteren, 1978).

This concept of citizenship is vital to local government because of the constitutional links between local and central government. Service users of the housing department are thus not only Council tenants and customers, but are stakeholders who can play an active role in the decision making process electing the Council and are owners of the authority's assets which are managed on their behalf.

The rights of citizens to Clarke and Stewart (1987b) are wide.

"Citizens are entitled

* to know the policies of the authority
* to know the decisions of the authority
* to know the reasons for the policies and the decisions of the authority
* to be able to debate and discuss the issues before the Council
* to have their voices heard on issues before the Council
* to have their interests and concerns weighed by the Council
* to be actively involved in the governing of the local community
* to be part of decision making
* to mould the work of the Council
* to judge the work of the Council
* to vote". (Clarke and Stewart, 1987(b))

PSO and Women's Issues

A second criticism made of PSO is the assumption that customers are a homogeneous mass, making the same demands on the authority and satisfied by the same services (Kettleborough, 1988). This is obviously not the case. Customers fall into a complex pattern of groupings which even themselves do not fully explain differing demands and expectations. An alternative to the homogeneous approach is to acknowledge this diversity through a personal approach which recognises the different needs of women in particular but also other under-represented groups in a service which has traditionally been dominated by white males. This involves ensuring that customer consultation considers issues relevant to these groups. Those conducting surveys need to consult from a basis of awareness. For women issues of access to the housing department resulting from poor public transport or the sexist remarks of repairs contractors who take advantage of the position of lone women in the home may be of equal importance to the complaints system and the Council's customer contract.

A similar series of arguments can be advanced about services for ethnic groups. In the past decade housing organisations have recognised the importance of providing information to customers in ethnic languages. Many authorities now provide information in the main ethnic languages of their district. Welsh districts and associations too have responded to the demands of their consumers providing written material in dual languages, Welsh and English.

Beyond Consumerism

The boundaries of PSO have been pushed further by Hambleton (1990 and 1991), who has developed Rhodes' concept of citizenship, arguing the importance of collective citizenship expressed as community development and the importance of the political dimension in local government.

The late 1980s have seen a continued struggle in central government about the political nature of its local counterpart. This has seen the abolition of tiers of local government, arguably for political ends. At the same time, government tried to resist proposals for strengthening local democracy contained in the Widdicombe Report by rejecting secondment of officers as political advisers. It has backed down, introducing such powers in the Local Government and Housing Act 1989, under which officers may be seconded to political parties to provide advice.

Emerging patterns of relationship between local authorities and their communities: a conceptual framework

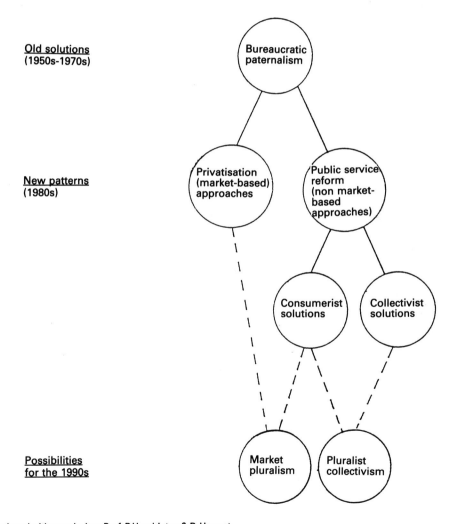

Reproduced with permission: Prof. R Hembleton & P. Hogget

This political dimension is particularly strong in housing, a service which dominates district councils in budget and staffing terms. It is an area which interests members, allowing them to pursue social policies and lobby for individual cases in an environment where technical knowledge is of less importance than in services like planning or environmental health.

In theory there is a clear division between the role of officers and elected members. As Hambleton notes (1990) "The dividing line between the professional/technical and the political has never been clear. It has always been a myth to suggest that members decide policy and officers implement it. Some members have always been interested in the detail of service delivery, while senior officers have always been influential in shaping overall strategy".

As central government continues to pursue a politically orientated rather than a consensus approach to policies, particularly with an anti-local government thrust, the politicisation of local government services is likely to grow. Labour councils thus seek not only to improve services for customers, but also to politicise their customers, giving both customer loyalty for housing and voter loyalty for Labour policies which resist the privatisation of local government services.

Customer Royal

While not rejecting the validity of the political environment of local government, or the complexity of public services, a second strand of the PSO debate has considered a path down which public services may continue to travel (Passmore 1991) in an effort to mirror the market and adopt a customer-orientated approach.

A number of specific weaknesses reduce the value of the word customer within public services. Firstly, many services are not available on customer demand, but are rationed on the basis of predetermined and published criteria. These criteria may be set down in law; the local authorities' requirements to consider housing need under Section 22 of the Housing Act 1985, or in policy such as a housing association's lettings policy. While many individuals will apply, few will be fortunate to receive an offer. It is argued that the customer has no power or choice in this situation.

A second complication is the multiplicity of users, whose goods may be in direct or partial conflict with one another. A neighbour dispute, or an estate improvement programme to a communal area illustrate this point of potential conflict.

These criticisms fail to undermine the argument that public services should pay more attention to the needs of their customers. It does however demand that public services consider how these dilemmas may be minimised.

These difficulties are not unique to the public sector. Private sector firms do manage such dilemmas; the British Airways flight which is fully booked, or the ten year waiting list for a Morgan car. These demonstrate that the theoretical view of the market, which supposedly offers choice to all customers at the point they need it, and planned provision of the public services, are not mutually exclusive.

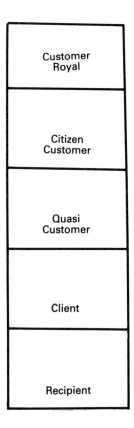

| Customer Royal |
| Citizen Customer |
| Quasi Customer |
| Client |
| Recipient |

The Customer Service Continuum

It is more helpful to consider the terms used to describe a customer as points along a continuum, which reflect the power relationship between the service user and the service provider.

The *first point* along the continuum may be termed *'recipients'*. At this point services are provided to the consumer who is in a low power position. The service supplier makes the decision of what and how much to supply, based purely on professional judgement, and considers that consultation is meaningless as the user will only consider their own needs and will fail to understand the broader picture.

The *second point* is that of *'client'*. Again the power of the service user is low and their role is passive. The provider bases decisions on professional judgement, although appreciates that the client has feelings, but believes they understand what these are without the need to consult.

A *third step* is *'Quasi customer'*; the service provider recognises users are not a homogeneous mass but hold a diversity of views. At this point, the provider may seek to gather these views through a survey and will use the data to change service delivery. However, the service user remains weak. There is little right of redress if the service provider fails to keep to published service standards. To enable quick and easy redress, a simple complaints/appeals channel is required. When these elements come together a commitment by the service provider to base resource decisions on service users' views, clear and explicit standards for each of the services provided and a simple right of redress, the *fourth stage* of *'Citizen Customer'* has been reached.

It is this stage which the Citizens' Charter initiative is encouraging providers to strive towards. Currently most housing organisations are struggling at steps two and three. A limited number of providers, however, have adopted simple complaints systems, consult customers regularly and are beginning to publish explicit customer contracts, which set out service standards.

The main weakness, however, is that the contract is not legally enforceable. The *final stage* in the continuum is only reached when customers who complain have an independent right of redress whose decision is binding on both parties, referred to as 'Customer Royal'. The current Ombudsman system is too slow, bureaucratic and lacking force to meet these requirements.

National Consumer Council

While the PSO debate has continued, and has become increasingly focused on local government provision, the National Consumer Council has adopted a hands-on approach, setting out a series of criteria by which public services may be evaluated (Potter 1988). These are as applicable to council housing or housing associations, as to the NHS or council planning service.

NCC offers 5 guiding principles to public services:

* access
* choice
* information
* redress
* representation.

The first principle is the granting of access. The decision of who shall have access to a public service, for example, who can join the waiting list, is a political one. Stakeholders, both users and others, have a right to know what criteria have been agreed and the basis for this decision. Once set, the second concern is that of accessibility. Do the criteria exclude groups who should be included? Are the criteria fair and just? Are young people, under 21 years, for example, excluded from the waiting list? Related to these conscious access restrictions, there may be unconscious restrictions; is information provided in local ethnic languages, are application forms easy to complete, is help available, are officers located in convenient or accessible locations?

The second principle of choice, is a difficult area for public services, and one which has traditionally been ignored. While it may be possible in parts of the service to provide choice; a choice of offers for rehousing or the colour of the bathroom suite in the improvement programme, in many parts of the service choice is not available. There is, for example, not a true choice of who is the landlord, in a housing environment where demand outstrips supply and attempts to offer choice such as the Housing Act 1988 provide only a one way ticket. In these situations partial substitutes may be available; easy access to a complaints system, external monitoring of service quality and fairness, and publication of performance indicators and service standards.

The third principle concerns the availability of information. There is a distinction between availability and provision. Providing such data to all in a flood may be of less value to users than making information publicly available. Publication encourages greater press and external scrutiny, enabling users to read a summary of key facts rather than wade through a detailed document.

The fourth principle is redress. Does the organisation have a simple complaints system? The NCC themselves recommend a graduated system. Research of local authority complaints procedures, however, revealed few authorities operated any system and those which did failed to operate a positive approach with complaint analysis feeding into a policy review (Serevirotne and Cracknell, 1988). There are signs that this is changing.

The final principle identified by Potter is that of representation. By definition there is representation in all public services, but this may be distanced through a number of filters. While in local government the relationship is clear, within the housing association movement the situation is more complex. Firstly, are associations public bodies? Strictly the answer is no, however they receive public funds, and are accountable for spending public money. This accountability is achieved through a number of filters; individual M.P.s are accountable to their electorate, including association tenants, and M.P.s monitor Government action. The Government has placed the resonsibility of monitoring associations with an agency, the Housing Corporation.

This distant relationship removes almost all of an individual's power to call their association to account through the democratic process. Alternative representation is required and the Corporation has rightly encouraged greater tenant participation.

Tenant participation is, however, sadly lacking in many associations, particularly at Management Committee and Sub-Committee level. The Corporation is attempting to tackle this problem by encouraging, at the point of registering new associations and during monitoring, greater tenant representation on Committees. A balance is needed though between users, potential users and those with the business skills to direct and control an organisation with thousands or millions of pounds of assets. A three way split between a business representative with finance and development skills, a community group, such as social services, women's aid, local council and tenants representatives may offer the most appropriate solution for many associations.

Principles of Public Service

The Citizens' Charter sets out six principles which public services should be expected to follow. Through these the Charter aims to "give citizens a better deal by extending consumer choice and widening competition. Whether the service is provided by the private sector or the public sector, the aim is to ensure that the citizen gets good service and good value for money".

The six principles are:

* standards
* information and openness
* choice and consultation
* courtesy and helpfulness
* putting things right
* value for money.

Labour too proposed a Citizens' Charter (Labour 1991), which was based upon the initiatives of a number of Labour controlled local councils who had implemented customer contracts, namely York D.C. and the L.B. of Lewisham. Labour's Charter was rights based and sought to empower citizens, by giving consumers a voice as well as the ability to hold service providers to account.

Labour's nine practical rights were:

* a right to choose
* a right to quality
* a right to safety
* a right to be treated equally
* a right to swift and fair redress
* a right to citizens' action
* a right to a voice
* a right to know
* a right to advocacy.

These proposed rights were to span public and private sectors, and were linked to specific legislative proposals under each heading. Citizens could expect legislation to protect home buyers under the 'right to know' by giving access to a housing log book, and improved access rights for disabled people under the proposals for equal treatment.

The implementation of the six principles of the Government's Charter is considered in relation to housing provision.

Standards

Customer Contracts

While the Government has encouraged public services to launch Charters detailing the services which are provided and standards of performance, in general these have been vague. The Patients' Charter avoids making specific promises about how quickly treatment will be provided.

Housing organisations have published information for customers at least since legislation demanded it in 1980, and the majority produced Tenants' Handbooks and leaflets on services before this. However, the majority of these were vague and failed to provide specific detailed guidelines of how long customers had to wait for a reply to a letter, or how quickly they would be seen when they went into the housing office.

The efforts of York, Lewisham and a small number of other Labour-controlled Councils began to change this, with the publication of service promises. These related to contractors' services initially; street cleaning, grounds maintenance and refuse collection. The customer contract usually explained the nature of the service contract which had been let, and, for example state; the day the bin would be collected, from where it should be collected and returned, plus telephone numbers for customer queries. In some instances, as in Lewisham, this was backed up by a compensation promise, that if the bin was not emptied a payment would be made to the customer.

These contracts have now spread to housing services. In York housing repairs and housing benefits contracts publicise standards, and other authorities such as East Northamptonshire and Welwyn Hatfield, have followed this route.

One of the main concerns is how the contract matches with other information supplied to tenants, possibly through a handbook. One way forward is for organisations to attempt to produce common standards for all their services, in relation to waiting times, complaints, publication of information on performance and appointments. This would form part of the standard tenants' handbook, which gave more general information on services, tenants' rights and an explanation of the tenancy agreement.

York's Contract for Housing Repairs

York's repairs contract for tenants was launched in March 1992, with a copy of the contract distributed to all Council tenants. It sets out repair standards for the service, mixing information which is also contained in York's Tenant Handbook with more detailed information on service delivery.

The contract promises:

* a negotiated appointment (am or pm) for all repairs with a target of no more than one week
* stated opening hours and contact number
* officers to give names and wear identity badges
* compensation for losses due to missed appointments and guarantee to do work within 24 hours
* to treat customers' homes with care, no use of radios and to clean up afterwards.

The East Northamptonshire DC – Advice Contract

This contract was launched as a supplement to Tenant information, as East Northamptonshire recognised the majority of advice team customers were private sector tenants and homeless applicants. The contract set out some basic standards of what customers using the advice service could expect. The contract set standards such as:

* maximum waiting times in reception
* maximum times for replies to correspondence
* maximum waiting time for non-emergency appointments
* customers to be provided with a summary of options available
* officers to give names in letters and in meetings
* officers to wear identity badges
* rights of appeal.

The setting of simple and tangible standards, and monitoring performance against them, aimed to give a clear signal to customers what they could expect.

Performance Standards

The Department of the Environment, along with the Welsh and Scottish Offices, has been keen to encourage both local authorities and housing associations to more closely consider their performance, and set forward targets at which to aim.

The concept of forward planning is not new, and was popular in the 1960s under a corporate planning model advocated by the Maud Committee. This strategic planning, however, both became too mechanistic as the pace of change grew and failed to seep through the hierarchy to operational targets.

Legislation, firstly affecting local government housing, and more recently local authorities in general, under the Citizens' Charter, now requires the publication of detailed information about services, and performance attainment.

Section 167 of the Local Government and Housing Act 1989, supplemented by two circulars, has set out an extensive scheme for English local authority housing departments of some 50 indicators. The indicators known as the Tenants Determination must be published annually between April-September and distributed to all secure tenants.

Indicators include:

* how many repairs they did and what type; response times, the capital programme and arrangements for maintenance work

* average weekly rents and rent payment methods; a breakdown of rent arrears by amount and period

* lettings details and allocations policy

* number of empty homes, why they are empty and average period that properties are empty

* number of homeless people accepted and number in temporary accommodation

* number of staff

* cost of housing service, broken down into headings.

In Wales a different implementation approach was adopted, which was less prescriptive and based on consultation (Smith and Walker 1993). The result has seen a gradual development of the system over the past three years, rather than a big bang.

While initial publications have focused on the performance of the individual authority, the Department of the Environment hopes authorities will begin to compare their performance over time and with neighbouring authorities. The Department of the Environment itself carried out a comparative exercise, and the data on performance is used by the Department in assessing authority performance for management under the Housing Investment Programme.

The scheme has been heavily criticised and we have considered these criticisms in detail elsewhere in this publication.

The Audit Commission too has produced its own scheme, as part of the Citizens' Charter. This requires local authorities to publish performance information annually in the local paper, on the full range of services they provide from Environmental Health to Planning and Finance. Housing departments are required to collect data which varies slightly to that under Section 167, although strangely there is little additional attention paid to community housing services, such as housing advice, waiting list and homelessness, rather than specific tenant information on arrears and voids.

While no legislative arrangements have been made for associations, outside of the Tenants' Guarantee, many are making an effort to provide performance information along the lines of the local authority schemes. Rather than produce vast quantities of graphs, charts and statistics, the focus is core data on arrears, voids and key policy issues.

There are more difficulties for associations in collecting and publishing this data. Estates are often scattered across a number of counties and possibly across the country, and performance may vary widely between regions depending on management control and social factors. To tackle this, regional statistics may be of more benefit, as the larger authorities themselves move towards estate and neighbourhood-based performance information.

Chartered Institute of Housing Management Standards

As part of its contribution to the quality debate, and to assist authorities in preparing competitive tendering specifications for housing services, the Chartered Institute of Housing has published recommendations for what it considers to be acceptable standards for Housing Management (CIH 1993).

The Institute acknowledges that although not all standards will be appropriate for every landlord, they will provide a useful benchmark for assessment and service reviews. In addition it is hoped by the Institute that private, as well as public, landlords will look to the standards as a model to follow in managing their own stock.

The publication includes standards for the following areas of housing services:

* customer care and information
* empty property management
* equal opportunity
* estate management
* homelessness services
* housing services for people with special needs
* rehousing services

* rent collection, accounting and arrears recovery
* rent setting and service charges
* repairs and maintenance
* tenant involvement.

In addition, key issues of equal opportunities, customer care and training which underpin the core standards are also the subject of recommendation.

Putting Things Right

The Right to Redress

The issue of a right to redress is one of the central principles of the Citizens' Charter. Customers must have access to a simple and effective procedure to highlight service failures which can be put right quickly.

Both local authorities and housing associations have been encouraged to recognise the importance of complaints procedures. The Local Ombudsman has previously advised local authorities that they should aim to resolve complaints internally and achieve this through well publicised and easy to follow complaints procedures. A failure to operate such an internal scheme in itself may lead to a finding of maladministration. The Housing Corporation has made a similar point in advising associations in 'Performance Standards' to adopt adequate procedures for dealing with complaints.

More recently, the Corporation has established an Ombudsman service for associations, one of the Citizens' Charter White Paper commitments. The initial emphasis, was on a system of intervention and investigation, rather than complaint resolution. However, following responses to the Housing Corporation's consultation paper, the system introduced seeks to offer arbitration as a first attempt at resolution. Where this fails a formal investigation may follow.

Despite this encouragement, local authorities and associations have both been slow to adopt appropriate mechanisms.

The Need for a Complaints System

The most common reasons expressed to us by managers for not adopting a formal system is that customers already complain and don't need encouragement. Research (HA Weekly) had revealed that one in six tenants do not complain even though they are dissatisfied. Further discussion on complaints usually reveals that those who do complain receive inconsistent treatment where procedures are not set out. For the landlord there are significant benefits in a formal mechanism being operated by all staff.

Firstly, a clearly set out procedure helps employees in performing their roles. They know what is their responsibility and know that support is available if the complaint becomes more serious. If the information is clear customers know who is responsible for that.

Secondly, customers will take reassurance if a complaints system is well publicised and past experience of dealing with the system demonstrates that a quick and satisfactory outcome can be achieved.

Thirdly, complaints offer an ideal opportunity for policy reviews where customer expectations have changed. The NCC has drawn attention to this benefit in particular when launching its report on good practice (NCC 1991).

"Tenants can feel stifled when it comes to expressing their views on the housing service they receive. If tenants don't complain, it's bad news for the housing organisation because it shuts off a valuable source of information about standards of performance". (Lady Wilcox, NCC Chair)

The report sets out good practice principles for social landlords to follow in establishing mechanisms for dealing with customer complaints. These are:

Conciliation

The primary objective of a system should be to promote conciliation, rather than confrontation. The outcome should enable all parties to feel the matter was dealt with fairly.

Positive Approach

The landlord should encourage complaints, and see the use of the mechanism as a potential benefit, rather than failure.

In Line with Rights

The procedure should reinforce statutory rights tenants hold through tenancy agreements and under legislation.

Easy to Use

Systems should be speedy, easy to use and well publicised. Staff should be familiar with the existence of the procedure and how it operates.

Fair and Impartial

Customers must see the system is fair and impartial. Those who operate the procedure must hold this aim as a central objective, and not be deflected by loyalty to the organisation or peer pressure.

Clearly Defined and Structured

The procedure and the customer information clearly define the steps involved and the scope of the procedure, what services it covers and what rights tenants have to go to the Ombudsman, local Councillors, M.P.s and Board Members.

Prompt

Procedure should enable complaints to be resolved at the lowest level and at the fastest speed. Customers should be kept informed of how long the process will take.

Publicity

The procedure should be publicised through a leaflet, available in offices, libraries, Citizens Advice Bureaux and other publications. The leaflet should clearly set out the steps involved.

Record Keeping

A record of all complaints should be kept. This provides a potential source for service review information and allows trends in complaints to be tracked.

The NCC recommend a formal procedure which landlords may wish to adopt.

		NCC Model	
Step	Who to Complain To	Action
Initial	Housing	Opportunity to resolve at primary customer contact point
Formal Complaints	Complaints Officer	Designated officer takes action to investigate, review decision and advise
Appeal	Senior Officer	Senior Officer reviews papers, policy and decision. Advises customer of outcome
Committee	Elected/ Committee Members	Committee/Sub-Committee review case
Beyond Organisation	MP/Housing Corporation/ Ombudsman	Customer directed to monitoring organisations.

Ombudsmen

Authorities have been slow to follow the NCC model. Those that have introduced systems for dealing with complaints have unfortunately fallen into the trap of confrontational approach, rather than conciliation.

This is one of the failures of the Ombudsman system itself. The Local Ombudsman places a heavy reliance on fact finding, rather than seeking a compromise between the parties in an ACAS style meeting. Partly as a result of this approach, complaints take, on average, a year to reach an outcome, and often leave complainants frustrated. This is because their claim is rejected, despite service failures as no maladministration took place, or because the result in their favour did not lead to a change in the Council's decisions. For the poor performing Councils, ignoring the Ombudsman is an option which too many still choose to follow.

The Housing Association Tenants' Ombudsman service has recognised many of these weaknesses and advocates a problem resolution approach, through conciliation or arbitration.

Alternatives

The NCC model is one which social landlords can adopt simply to deal with tenants' complaints and add flair by gifts of flowers to customers where things have gone badly wrong (Miller), or offer compensation although, as the Citizens' Charter acknowledges, customers want a service not compensation for not receiving the service.

The external systems of M.P. and Ombudsman, however, require review, M.P. intervention on cases often leads to the case receiving additional priority which, on merit, it may not deserve. Alternatively, in the case of genuine complaints of service, M.P.s have no power to ensure the matter is resolved. This should be the job of the Local Ombudsman but the failures of this service have been highlighted already.

The alternative would be for the Local Ombudsman service to change its approach in housing to a face to face conciliation meeting, in the ACAS style. The Ombudsman meets both parties, individually reviews the papers and legislation relating to the case before a joint meeting to establish an agreement. Where this aim is achieved, both parties sign an agreement. Where no joint agreement can be reached the Ombudsman makes a decision which is binding on both parties.

Information and Openness

There is some overlap between the six principles of the Citizens' Charter. The right to information adds little to the principles of standards and publication. The Council Tenants' Charter fails to go into any more detail than setting out the rights which are already available to Council tenants. These are:

* a right to have a copy of the summary of the Council's rules on letting homes

* a right to look at a full set of the rules for letting homes

* a right to have a copy of the rules of the tenancy

* a right to attend Council Committee meetings and see minutes

* a right to have access to personal records.

Access to Personal Files

These rights have in the main, been available to tenants since 1980, with the exception of a right to see one's personal file. This right was introduced in 1989, under 'The Access to Personal Files (Housing) Regulations', although landlords may charge for this information. The Data Protection Act gives similar rights to those wishing to view computer records. Few tenants, however, use these rights, possibly because landlords give little publicity about them.

Meetings

While Council tenants have access to Committee meetings, this is limited to a passive role, listening to discussion and reading papers presented. There is a further right to read relevant background papers listed on the public report, although little use is made of this.

As a result of meetings being opened up, much of the decision making has retreated to private meetings, either formally at Sub-Committee level or briefing sessions which there is no right to attend. The majority of Council Committees are a rubber stamping exercise, with officers and members aware of the major decisions which will be taken in advance.

Tenants' Handbooks

The most common form of customer information to tenants is a handbook. This traditionally explains the landlord's tenancy agreement, and provides information on services plus contact numbers.

Handbooks fall into three general formats:

*   fixed booklet
*   leaflets in a pack
*   ring binder.

Each option offers attractions as a model format, and tenants' views are likely to be split as to which option is most attractive.

Handbook Options		
Type	**Advantages**	**Disadvantages**
Booklet	* lower cost per unit * all information in one place	* difficult to update
Leaflet	* easy to update and add to	* tenants unsure if they have all the information * updated leaflets may not be added to set sent to tenant
Ring Binder pages	* easy to update * professional/ upmarket image	* tenants unsure if they have all the information * updated pages may not be added * higher production cost

The weakness with the written word is that a proportion of the population have either a low reading age or are unable to read. As social housing becomes even more marginalised, this is a greater problem for landlords to address. One method is to provide audio cassettes, which are an accessible medium for both those untrained in reading, as well as those who have a visual disability.

'Good practice Councils' are now taking the initiative further by offering to translate any material into ethnic languages, and, in some cases, to braille for customers.

Welsh authorities operating in a dual language environment now provide customer information in both English and Welsh, although the number of Welsh speakers remains at less than 20% of the population, and falling.

Consultation and Choice

Consultation Rights

Social housing customers have a legal right to be consulted, unlike the users of many other public services. Council tenants have a statutory right under the Housing Act 1985, Section 105 to be consulted about a "matter of housing management". The authority needs to advise the tenant of its proposals, give notice enabling tenants to respond within a reasonable period and to consider these views in reaching its decision. A number of limitations have been placed on this right.

Firstly, the section does not relate to rent increases. Secondly, the change needs to be 'substantial'. It has been argued by some authorities that voluntary tendering on a housing management contract to a private management agent was not a 'substantial' change and, as such, no consultation was required. The Department of the Environment was concerned that CCT legislation may be exposed to potential tenant veto and an amendment to Section 105 was included in the Housing and Urban Development Act 1993.

Housing associations assured tenants benefit from similar rights to the original Section 105, contained in the Tenant's Guarantee.

Both local authorities and housing associations have sought independently to improve tenant involvement with the support of the Department of the Environment and the Housing Corporation.

TPAS Model

TPAS have developed a simple model to describe the range of consultation strategies which landlords may employ. The model is based on Arnstein's ladder of community participation. At the level of least participation the landlord tells the tenant of the decisions which have been made. As involvement increases the landlord seeks the views of tenants and finally at the highest level of participation tenants have the right to make decisions on a full range of issues.

Urban Participation Initiative

Islington embarked upon a programme of decentralisation in 1985, seeking to both physically decentralise service delivery and decision making, and to involve the community in the decision making process.

Physical decentralisation was achieved by the construction of local offices, which look more like pizza huts than the traditional municipal buildings. Decision making has now become part of neighbourhood forums, which have an advisory role to the Council's central committees.

TENANTS HAVE THE RIGHT TO MAKE DECISIONS ON A FULL
RANGE OF ISSUES

TENANTS HAVE A RIGHT TO MAKE SOME DECISIONS

TENANTS HAVE GENUINE OPPORTUNITIES TO INFLUENCE
DECISIONS

LANDLORDS SEEK TENANTS VIEWS WHEN MAKING DECISIONS

LANDLORDS EXPLAIN DECISIONS TO TENANTS

LANDLORD TELLS TENANTS THE DECISIONS MADE

Housing matters are dealt with by both Forums and local housing sub-committees. Representatives from local tenant associations participate in meeting. In addition, to broaden the focus of the neighbourhood groups, Tenant Liaison Forums are held, at which tenant representatives are able to present matters which have not been resolved at the local level. Tenants also sit as non voting members of the Housing Committee.

The Council does set down a code of conduct, which Forums must follow if they are to receive funding. The code refers to the Council's equal opportunities policy, recommending the provision of creches, transport and translation services.

The result has been that after eight years the Council is acknowledged as 'one of the pioneering authorities in developing tenant participation' (District Auditor Service). The Council is however keen to continue its efforts to get tenants involved, through the 95 tenants' associations which exist. In the Council's 1993/94 Housing Investment bid the document pledges support for a second Estate Management Board, and is negotiating with 40 estates over formal management agreements, defining service standards.

Rural Participation Initiative

Wherry HA was the fourth successful large scale voluntary transfer, completing the transfer in April 1990. The Association acquired 3700 homes from Broadland DC, and have subsequently built 300 new homes, in partnership with Broadland and three other district councils in East Anglia.

As part of the transfer process the Association built up relationships with residents, which following transfer Wherry have sought to enhance through the development of resident democracy.

Resident democracy was developed by law in the management of social housing in Denmark during the 1970s. The approach has three broad aims:

* to allow tenants to be directly involved in the setting of service specifications, rent levels and conditions of tenancy in relation to a particular estate.

* to define the rights and responsibilities of landlords and tenants more clearly, but to leave full responsibility for providing services with the landlord.

* to develop a more equal partnership between landlord and tenant by making service delivery accountable to tenants.

The approach works at the local level by creating community identity. Residents create and work through a local management board made up of tenants and leaseholders elected from the estate. The local manager reports regularly to the board, agreeing changes in service provision and cost.

Wherry has selected two rural parishes to pilot the approach; Cawston, containing 126 homes, and Reepham area containing 183 homes. In each area progress has been made through small working groups, with a wider group of residents kept informed through a newsletter and periodic meetings.

The outcome has been a series of specifications defining service standards for:

* repairs and maintenance
* landscape maintenance
* void control
* warden service
* arrears counselling and control
* enforcing tenancy conditions
* support to the Board.

Despite its rural location the pilot schemes have successfully been implemented. Elsewhere in the country, at South Somerset and Sutton LBC, the initiative is also being pursued with the assistance of Aldbourne Associates and Arbejdernes Kooperative Byggeforening, a Danish housing association.

Choice

The Charter argues that public services should also provide choice to customers 'wherever practicable'. While this sounds appealing, it is far from practicable. In social housing the product is rationed, the cost of switching from one home to another is expensive for tenant and landlord, tenants face removal fees and the landlord must carry out as a minimum health and safety checks before reletting. When properties change ownership, as in the case of a stock transfer, large fees are encountered; valuation, property survey plus land registry and taxation.

This does not rule out choice, however, and social landlords, during the 1990s, need to look at mechanisms to provide greater choice to their customers.

Areas of Choice		*Choices*
(i)	Rent	Method of payment Which service standard/rent category
(ii)	Repairs	Which service standard Which contractor What time – appointments
(iii)	Involvement	Level of involvement/self management
(iv)	Improvement	Which improvements i.e. colours/units/systems Which contractor

Tenants do have some choice over rent payment methods, but varying service levels may be an option to be explored. Under this arrangement tenants could opt for an enhanced service for which a higher rent payment was due. The enhanced service may offer a fuller repairs service including internal decorating. The repairs service itself could offer customer choice over the time when contractors will call and which contractor off the appointed list will carry out the work. York City and Leicester have already made preliminary steps to offer appointments to customers, giving a choice of morning or afternoon calls on a specified day. The public utilities have gone further by offering 4 appointment slots for the day.

With work being carried out which may not have been precisely defined when the job was reported, this may be as precise as public housing can get. The aim, however, should remain a specific fixed time.

While social landlords are striving towards these objectives, other efforts undermine the provision of choice. CCT offered the potential for consumer involvement. Tenants could have weighed up costs versus quality issues and made decisions about who managed their homes. The failure to allow tenant choice in this area reveals the dominance of 'value for money' among the principles of public service set under the Charter.

Helpfulness and Courtesy

Helpfulness

Under the banner of helpfulness comes an array of ideas and strategies which fall outside the other five principles. Within this principle the Charter considers a span from equal opportunities through to name badges. It is this area which is most often considered 'customer care' when authorities implement service improvements.

At its most basic level the efforts of Leicester's customer care code and Reading's guide to customer care tell customers and staff the standards which the Council aims to deliver.

CASE STUDIES

Leicester Customer Care Code

Leicester sets out nine conditions which it aims to maintain at all times:

* we will be friendly and helpful at all times
* we will deal with all enquiries quickly
* we will make our replies easy to understand
* we will keep appointments

* we will make sure you know all your rights
* we will carry out our duties, especially repairs, and always protect your property
* we accept your right to complain and guarantee a full investigation and response
* we will ask you to assess all the services we provide for you
* we will provide a sensitive housing service for all customers.

Reading Customer Care

Reading's publication on customer care provides a simple guide for staff to reinforce a training message that customers matter. Under 'Making people welcome' it suggests:

* welcome them with a smile and ask if you can help
* use their name
* use a pleasant tone of voice
* be polite and keep calm
* mind your body language
* stay clear of jargon
* always listen carefully
* try and find an answer to the question
* give them your name
* do what you said you were going to do.

Customer care, however, is not the full extent of customer service or Citizens' Charter initiatives, only one part. By failing to consider the basics, the service remains unchanged at the point of contact with customers. Equally ignoring deep rooted change, as is common, leaves the customer contact staff struggling within an unsupportive organisation.

A mix of local authorities and associations have been able to bring together the diverse elements in the way we have suggested in this chapter. They have integrated customer service into a broader management strategy which seems to manage change in the complex and dynamic world of social housing.

Braintree District Council

Braintree's efforts to implement culture change towards a philosophy of 'quality local government services' dates back to 1983. This change followed the appointment of a new Chief Executive who recognised the need within local government for a more externally orientated, dynamic, action-centred management style.

Early effort was placed on three core areas. Firstly, establishing improved accountability by introducing a systematic and integrated management system.

Secondly, encouraging employees to focus on outcomes, the delivery of the service to customers, rather than placing primary interest in the process. Thirdly, the authority sought to create a management style and corporate vision which was appropriate.

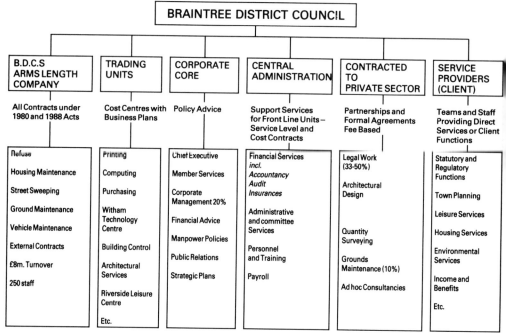

Braintree's flexible model
Reproduced from 'Total Management' Braintree D.C.

CORPORATE STRATEGY

MISSION/VISION
CORPORATE STRATEGY
SERVICE STRATEGIES
HIPS Local Plan Recreation Manpower, etc.

COMMITTEE ANNUAL PLANS
SERVICE/BUSINESS PLANS
COMMITTEE TARGETS
INDIVIDUAL TARGETS/PERFORMANCE APPRAISAL

Braintree framework for Corporate Strategy
Reproduced from 'Total Management' Braintree D.C.

The authority developed during the 1980s a vision statement centred on the slogan 'Braintree Means Business' and linked this to a set of core values.

Core Values

* we are customer orientated
* we believe in the abilities of the individual
* we must be responsive and responsible
* we believe in quality
* we are action orientated.

Vision Statement

The vision is of a District which:

* is prosperous, clean and socially balanced;

* meets the basic needs of all in our community for affordable housing and a range of housing choices, for worthwhile employment and for security, health and welfare services and personal mobility;

* retains, respects and enhances its attractive environment particularly its countryside, villages, historic buildings and conservation areas;

* whilst retaining its traditional character provides a range of modern industry on quality business parks, encourages initiatives and enterprise as well as quality shopping, arts, leisure, education and welfare facilities;

* has thriving town centres at Braintree, Withen and Halstead; town centres which are safe, convenient, accessible and attractive to shoppers and those who live and work there;

* meets the demands for efficient movement of road traffic, but not at the expense of safety and environmental conditions (particularly in towns and villages) or the neglect of public transport;

* meets the particular leisure, welfare and housing needs of the young and the elderly; and

* exhibits a real pride and respect on the part of all sections of the community, public and private, in its surroundings, with clean and tidy streets, parks and open spaces and property that is well maintained.

The strategy clarifies the corporate culture, management and employee development. More importantly the strategy seeks to provide a link between each tier of the strategic process, from vision to operational service, each underpinned by quality customer service.

Having created an integrated planning style, the implementation of the process was based on communication and training. This aspect is the most difficult for any organisation and where most fail to achieve success. But it is here that Braintree's ten years of effort have borne fruit. A study by Ashridge Management College (Wille 1992) revealed a high level of employee understanding of corporate aims and, more importantly, a commitment by staff to achieve these aims.

The Council was further complimented for its efforts to pursue a 'company wide' BS5750 accreditation. By the start of 1992 only three organisations in the U.K. had achieved this, none of whom operated in the public sector. While an expensive strategy, estimated to cost approximately £100,000 in total to achieve full accreditation, the authority believes this brings benefits not only in service quality but as an improved defence against competition in the CCT environment which faces housing and other white collar services as well as manual services affected by the 1988 legislation.

The crowning glory, however, for the housing service was the award in 1992 of the Charter Mark for the Council's housing management and rural initiatives. The authority was able to demonstrate its achievements against the *Charter Mark's seven criteria:*

* publication of service standards
* customer consultation
* clear customer information
* courteous and efficient staff
* efficient complaints system
* independent validation of performance
* innovation.

While in its public message from senior managers Braintree is no different from fifty or more authorities who are actively pursuing customer orientated services, its implementation differentiates Braintree and a handful of others from the masses. This small core of authorities have succeeded in making the leap from innovative concepts to effective customer orientation which is recognised and appreciated by their customers.

Wrekin Council

Introduction

Wrekin's approach to customer service has been a model for Public Service

Orientation. Its focus has been internal and external change, in recognition that high quality service requires a high level of employee involvement. Over the past decade Wrekin have both successfully managed this change, and managed the changes in their external environment.

The Council covers a large area, with a mix of urban and rural population totalling 130,000. It employs over 1,200 staff within the organisation, divided between service departments and central support departments.

The drive for change, as so often occurs, was stimulated by the arrival of a new Chief Executive and Personnel Manager in the early 1980s. A review of the organisation structure and strategy lead to the creation of a corporate culture based upon 3 core values; quality, caring and fairness. This approach has been supported by a range of initiatives based on research findings.

Attitude Survey

In 1987 Wrekin undertook the first of what has become an annual survey of resident attitudes. The MORI survey covered a 1.5% sample of households drawn from across the district. It sought to measure the Council's performance across the range of its services, what priorities people had, opinions of local and central government, the Council's image and the availability of information.

While the original survey provided valuable information, it provoked as many questions as it answered. It was a snap shot of what was happening rather than an effective measure of services.

As an immediate follow-up, several customer attitude surveys were launched in individual service areas to clarify areas of concern and test out options for change.

The survey did, however, impact directly on policy and played a part in the design of the Council's first local shop. These local shops were an effort by the Council to move out of the Civic Offices and into the community. Inter-agency problems were also identified, as residents found difficulty in distinguishing between County and District services. With a positive commitment from elected members to raise the district's profile, the strategy may also bring significant benefits in local government reorganisation, when residents consider at what level their local Council should operate.

At the operational level, the housing repairs service was criticised for being too slow and relying too heavily on cyclical maintenance. Changes to repairs were quickly put in place, moving towards a greater reliance on a responsive service favoured by tenants.

Annual surveys now track trends in service delivery and provide feedback to the strategic planning undertaken by the Council in advance of budget preparation. The problem with surveys of this kind is the lead time between collection of survey data, which may be June-August, and service changes which may not take effect until 9 months later. Such a delay would be unthinkable in Mars' or McDonald's product range. However, the democratic process is slow, requiring several Committee cycles to note the results, select options, approve budget, agree revised policy and implement.

Employee Care

The Council's approach is that it aims to be both model employer and the best employer in the local market. As a result of offering the best it has high expectations of its staff. The Council's employee strategy has four elements; core values, recruitment and induction, staff development and training and information.

Reinforcing understanding of core values is at the heart of the Council's approach. Wrekin believe all employees should be aware of, and understand, the Council's key objectives and the values which underpin the process of achieving these objectives.

As a 'model' employer the Council wishes to attract the right employees. Rather than placing a heavy reliance solely on interview, Wrekin have developed a range of assessment techniques for posts throughout the organisation. These test skills required in the job and range from simple tests for junior posts through to psychometric tests and presentations for more senior posts. The wish to broaden the assessment basis and consider a wider range of information than interview performance takes time, but the Council believes this is time well spent if the employee works with the organisation for the next 10 years.

Having recruited staff, there is attention to developing them. The starting point for all employees is an induction programme, which assists employees to start building a network of colleagues across the organisation and to understand the Council's functions, its values and its objectives. This continues in a more formal development programme involving individual counselling to staff on career aspirations and secondments to other departments to build practical skills and assist in the network development.

Training, too, has taken a high profile, and is well resourced. Employees spend days in service reviews, examining the service they provide, identifying barriers and seeking improvement plans. In addition, basic skills training on communications is provided in-house. The final component is information. Communication within the Council is recognised as a priority. Two major means are used to disseminate information; team briefing and the employee newsletter.

Team meetings are used to cascade a central brief through the organisation within the space of a few days, with departmental and with team information added as it flows down the organisation. By the time Chief Officer Team information reaches customer contact staff it makes up less than 10% of the total information. The focus at team level begins local team issues and a percentage of department issues.

To complement the team briefing an employee newsletter is published. It provides a forum to publicise jobs, corporation news and staff matters which would not come through team briefing.

Quality, Caring, Fairness

The corporate values underpin the activities throughout the organisation. By being simple there is little need to change away from these as the external environment changes. Corporate objectives may need to change over time, and Wrekin has not ignored the environment in which they are operating, whilst also considering the customers which they serve.

York City

While a number of authorities have pursued customer services strategies more actively in some departments than others, York City has been successful in balancing the need for autonomy with an acceptance that customers are only interested in the service, not the bureaucracy which the organisation creates to provide the service.

York has pioneered the use of customer contracts in local authorities and its early work in this area during the late 1980s laid much of the foundation for the Government's own Citizens' Charter.

At the centre is the customer who needs to be:

* informed
* involved
* offered choice.

Customer information is provided through a quarterly newsletter, recently re-launched in full colour. This is complemented by a range of leaflets on services, a tenants' handbook and customer contracts. The contracts set out service standards. The first ones, on street cleaning and refuse, were unique as users of these services have previously been neglected in terms of what services may be expected. More recently, housing repairs and benefits contracts have been produced. These set out timescales and explain priorities, and offer more information than housing services have been used to providing.

The Council annually issues a Citizens' Charter which explains past performance and future ambitions. The Audit Commission's indicators for local authorities now make it compulsory for all authorities to publish similar data on an annual basis.

To complement information, York has actively sought to encourage tenant participation. It now has 92% of tenants represented by the 17 residents' associations city wide. These are supported by community advisers, who help organise meetings and can organise training and arrange typing. These groups, along with Tenant Review Boards, which are set up during modernisation schemes as a tenants' watchdog, ensure tenant involvement in the management process.

The strongest message from tenants was on the issue of choice. Tenants did not just want to be informed or involved, they wanted to choose. York offers tenants a choice of colours, bathroom and kitchen suites and of which contractor does the work. The result has been significant improvement in tenant satisfaction, as tenants feel that they have specified the work and acted as quality controller. Satisfaction with the overall service has increased by 22% to 86%.

These efforts to monitor customer satisfaction in modernisation, cascade through the remainder of the service with an annual service monitor. Rather than noting totals in each category, York compares its performance over time, tracking responses to specific areas and seeking to identify key reasons for dissatisfaction. Where these are outside of the Council's control, an information response through leaflet and newsletters can help to adjust customer expectations. Where the problem is within York's influence, direct action can be taken. The survey has impacted on repairs policies, empty properties, allocations and planned maintenance.

The third strand is the constant policy review which, while creating a sense of trickle change in the department rather than stability, has brought both innovation and service improvements.

The repairs appointment system overcame complaints expressed by customers that they did not know when contractors would call. The housing department now negotiates directly with the customer to agree a convenient time for the work on non-emergency jobs. If the contractor fails to keep the appointment, customers are promised the work will be carried out within 24 hours at a time convenient to them, including evenings and weekends.

As a result of the system York claim repair response times have been reduced by over 50%, and contractors are making savings of £26,000 per annum, because they no longer waste time on abortive calls.

Staff training has taken a high priority. All staff receive a morning reception on their first day, which spells out the golden rules of good service, from a reminder that customers pay the wages to replying to letters in 10 working days. A formal induction to the Council is held every three months.

Training continues during an hour of early closing, which provides the opportunity for workshop sessions run by specialist staff and managers on subjects from plain English to rent arrears control and welfare benefits for beginners.

Like the other good practice organisations, York relies on team briefing to update its staff on what's going on in the Council and conducts staff attitude surveys.

Information gathering from staff has been formalised through staff workshops, which operate in a similar way to quality circles. Suggestions from these sessions have resulted in an upgrading of recetion area, with leaflet racks, magazines and children's toys provided. Areas of confusion, such as who maintains tenant-fitted gas fires, have also been sorted out and procedures made simpler.

The final strand of York's approach can be summarised as a partnership; a partnership between members and managers, the Council and its employees and between the Council and its customers.

Summary

- Public services need to recognise they exist to provide services for people, and the service is only of value if valued by customers. These customers are the test of quality.

- Local government has specific dilemmas in managing in both a market and a political environment. This requires government to view users as both customers and citizens.

- A common series of principles are emerging which can be used to assess service quality; standards, information and openness, choice and consultation, courtesy and helpfulness, putting things right and value for money.

CHAPTER 6: BALANCING CUSTOMER NEEDS

Introduction

This chapter aims to:

- identify the difficulties of a multi-customer multi-provider environment

- identify the primary providers and consider the needs of their customers

- offer simple mechanisms to deal with this conflict between competing customer priorities.

Who are the Customers?

For social housing providers the relationship between supplier and customer is not simple. Social housing has more than a single customer, and the roles of the 'provider' overlap. While for housing associations the situation remains stable, CCT has injected a new perspective which local authorities need to consider. Local authority housing departments can no longer talk about meeting the needs of their customers; the tenants.

The changing role of authorities from provider to purchaser, and the fragmentation to client, contractor and strategist ends the one to one relationship between landlord and tenant. In its place is the multi-party relationship of the new housing manager trinity; client, contractor and strategist. This chapter considers the difficulties of communicating with customers in a multi-stakeholder, multi-provider market, and in particular the CCT environment.

Client Services

The client function within housing remains at an early stage of development. The Department of the Environment has provided guidelines of the split of services, but until the first contracts have been let, performed and evaluated ready for the second contract period, the learning curve remains steep.

Much work has already gone into assisting authorities to prepare for CCT with the publication of the ADC/CIH guidance manual on competition within local

Client/Contractor hard and soft split

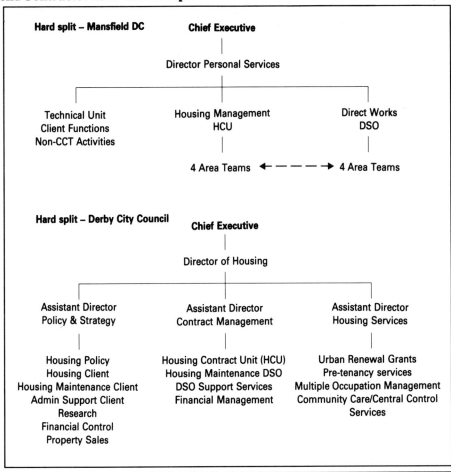

Hard split – Mansfield DC   **Chief Executive**

Director Personal Services

Technical Unit Client Functions Non-CCT Activities	Housing Management HCU	Direct Works DSO

4 Area Teams ←– – –→ 4 Area Teams

Hard split – Derby City Council   **Chief Executive**

Director of Housing

Assistant Director Policy & Strategy	Assistant Director Contract Management	Assistant Director Housing Services
Housing Policy Housing Client Housing Maintenance Client Admin Support Client Research Financial Control Property Sales	Housing Contract Unit (HCU) Housing Maintenance DSO DSO Support Services Financial Management	Urban Renewal Grants Pre-tenancy services Multiple Occupation Management Community Care/Central Control Services

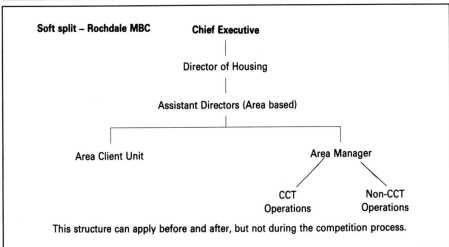

Soft split – Rochdale MBC   **Chief Executive**

Director of Housing

Assistant Directors (Area based)

Area Client Unit   Area Manager

CCT Operations   Non-CCT Operations

This structure can apply before and after, but not during the competition process.

Source: 'Competition and local authority housing services' The pilot experience: Report Two (ADC/CIH) authority housing services. This has been aided by the work of the 7 pilot authorities; Derby, East Staffordshire, Mansfield, Mid Suffolk, LB Newham, Rochdale and Westminster.

However, in performing this client role, authorities need to consider who are their customers. The client's primary function is to:

* define services
* determine service standards and procedures
* determine how different contractors work together
* prepare contract documentation
* tender and award the contract
* monitor contract performance against standards.

For the client, the stakeholder group is broadly similar to the pre-CCT/enabling stakeholder group:

* tenants
* elected members – Housing Committee
* Department of the Environment.

The three stakeholders, while not perceived as customers, each have influence and each provide or influence funding through housing subsidy in the case of the Department of the Environment, recommendations to Council from Housing Committee and the statutory rights of tenants to be consulted over matters which affect their home.

The mechanisms for involving and consulting these groups in the latter two cases exist. The Department of the Environment has laid down explicit consultation procedures for HIP and issues guidelines; the Council has delegated its functions on housing management to the Committee. Tenant involvement however may be more difficult to manage within a CCT environment.

Tenants' views will be sought by the client to assist them in contract preparation, particularly in defining and determining service standards. However, in small district councils the benefits of CCT will be costly. If CCT is to offer any saving, few staff will be available to undertake detailed tenant consultation.

The client is also likely to look to tenants to assist in monitoring the contractor. This may be through employing 'mystery callers'. These mystery tenants will monitor contracts they have with the service:

* how long did it take to get a reply to a letter
* how long was the wait in the reception area
* are staff polite
* how long did it take to get the housing repair done.

This technique is commonly used in the hotel and travel business. In this sector hotel chains hire individuals to visit one hotel/restaurant a month and report back on the findings to the head office. The system enables real time monitoring at a minimum cost.

The hotel only finds out they have had a mystery caller when they receive a report from headquarters.

The mystery caller offers a cost effective mechanism to monitor service contracts, and provides an opportunity to involve in the monitoring process customers who bring their own standards and expectations. It is these standards, rather than artificially created and monitored standards which the client and their professional staff develop, which are the real time measure of service quality.

An alternative monitoring approach which has been developed by clients in cleansing contracts is the use of consultants to act as the 'mystery caller'. As part of their approach to environmental campaigning, the Tidy Britain Group offer spot monitoring to local authorities as part of their campaign package. Authorities end up with periodic reports on the cleanliness of their district ranked under Environment Protection Act standards.

In housing, getting inside the service is more difficult. The service and its failures are less obvious than in street cleaning or refuse collection. Tenants are likely to be the only individuals who will be able to monitor, unbeknown to the contractor, the service standard as it is delivered. Whether local authority clients seize this opportunity to more actively involve tenants in the contract process remains to be seen.

Contractor Services

It has been suggested that authorities need not worry about CCT as services will stay in house. While this is largely true for the first round of tendering, subsequent rounds will see an ever increasing number of competitors and contracts being provided externally. This will, in part, come from authority policy to externalise services and in part from the authority's failure to win the tender.

Based upon the experience of Rutland, Westminster and Brent competition is likely to come from:

*   estate agents
*   consultants
*   housing associations.

Other sectors may emerge including management buy outs (MBO), and construction companies. European managers have also expressed interest from social housing providers in the Netherlands to French water companies.

The contractor role is possibly simpler, although the tender process carries considerable risk and demands a high degree of experience. The contractor's primary function will be:

*   obtain information on the contract
*   prepare and submit a tender
*   set up their operation to meet the specification
*   operate the contract
*   monitor costs and service levels.

This may include self monitoring procedures and contracts may also encourage contractors to define their own quality standards, above the stated minimum, which would be evaluated at the tender evaluation stage along with price.

The contractor will have no requirement to consider a wide group of multiple stakeholders. These stakeholders may be limited to the client or, if a DSO, will also include the DSO Board. For the contractor, the needs of the tenant are unimportant. Only the views and needs of the client will be considered. Tenants' views will only be considered of importance when they are endorsed by the client.

Rutland's decision to voluntarily tender reveals this differential. The District Council chose not to consult tenants under Sections 27 or 105 Housing Act 1985, which were due to be amended by the Leasehold Reform Housing and Urban Development Act 1993. Despite the legal uncertainty surrounding this decision, contractors from the voluntary housing movement and private sector were able to proceed to tender. As one of the tenderers remarked, "if the Council pays the piper, they call the tune, not the tenants".

The general rule has been for the client to include in the contract, mechanisms for monitoring contract quality. One of these is tenant satisfaction, and a rolling survey of tenants' views, with the results reported to the contract monitoring meeting and client access to original data. This gives a sharper focus to the importance of tenants' needs than a requirement in the contract for BS5750 or the publication of the contractor's customer care policy.

This area of contract quality monitoring is one area in which the DSO contractors have an opportunity to differentiate themselves from the competitors, or meet client requirements which a new external contractor may have difficulty pricing or performing (Passmore 1992). Many of the good practice ideas in this publication offer this differentiation opportunity.

Housing Strategist

While client and contractor may be considered to be hand in glove, the strategist takes a broader view of housing than tenants. The strategist's objectives may include:

* identifying housing priorities
* devising strategies for addressing priorities
* monitoring housing environment.

For the strategist, a role new to housing in the late 1980s, is the potential to be the lead partner of the housing manager trinity. It is the strategist who prepares the Housing Investment Programme (HIP) bid, liaises with associations on Housing Association Grant (HAG) bids, plans the capital programme and may also take responsibility for housing research/policy as well as retained services such as housing advice and homelessness. The broad range of functions is reflected in the multiple stakeholders who the strategist may consider to be a 'customer':

* Council tenants
* housing associations
* housing applicants
* homeless households
* Department of the Environment
* Housing Corporation
* other housing players in the district – i.e., estate agents and land owners
* elected members – Housing and Policy and Resources Committees.

This wide-ranging list identifies a potential difficulty for the strategist in consulting and involving customers in the work of planning the district's strategic housing plans.

We have already referred to the Department of the Environment's encouragement to local authorities for them to more actively involve other interested parties in planning the Housing Investment Programme.

In managing the housing manager trinity local authorities have responded in different ways. Among the pilot authorities most favour a formal division between client and contractor, but retaining both within a single department. This approach is particularly important to the smaller authorities, who are able to let a single contract. With fewer staff, a split is likely to increase staff costs, with little real gain.

The models advocated by the ADC/CIH manual reveal a range of possible structures to manage these competing customer needs. The manual however marginalises the role of the strategist. Yet it is this role which the new unitary authorities are most likely to consider of pivotal importance. With larger housing stocks, the focus on operational issues is likely to diminish, as members focus on overview issues of policy and strategy to address housing need.

Case Study – Derby City – HIP Consultation

In preparing its 1993/94 Housing Investment Programme bid the City Council worked hard to include all the key players during the development process. These include traditional groups such as the Housing Corporation, DOE, housing associations and tenants, as well as less traditional groups such as the health authority, training agencies, voluntary organisations and customer panels.

The Council currently consults 16 customer panels, and intends to set up 14 further panels across the remainder of the City. The panels provide a formal mechanism, complementing existing tenants' groups. In addition the homeless, ethnic minorities and disabled customers have an opportunity to input into Council decisions through their own forum meetings.

While comprehensive the difficulties of resolving conflicting stakeholder priorities remain. The City Council attempts to minimise these through setting out statutory obligations and its own priorities based on need.

Bids

A similar approach can be taken by the strategist to the HAG bids, if group liaison arrangements exist with the local associations. The importance, however, of such consultation will be reduced as the HIP comes to include the Housing Corporation funding.

These strategic planning functions illustrate the dilemma of the strategist who is faced with competing demands from groups. Each group has data to support its case for funding, but the ultimate priorities must be set by the Council. The conflict between stakeholders is picked up by the section below.

For other aspects of the strategist's work, basic service delivery consultation is required. For some customer groups this is more difficult and little thought has previously been given to monitoring customer satisfaction of housing advice or homelessness services. This is equally true of other non-Housing Revenue Account services; improvement grants and care and repair schemes.

Housing Association Environment

Housing associations have traditionally seen local authorities as their customers, along with the Housing Corporation. This development led view, based on funding, is beginning to change as greater attention is placed on housing management service quality.

The customers served by development and housing management are likely to have different priorities. The attention to tackling housing need without reflecting on management implications reveals larger associations' obsession with growth at all cost. 'Building Communities' (Page 1993) criticised this approach.

With grant rates declining and rents on new developments rising well above the NFHA affordability target, associations face several choices. Should the association stop developing, as successful development can only be achieved by forcing up rents on existing developments to subsidise new rents? Are existing tenants of greater priority than the association's contribution towards tackling housing need? These questions are forcing a growing tension in the housing association movement.

Increasingly associations are consulting their tenants; individually through surveys of individual services, random annual sample surveys to track performance year on year and through residents' associations.

Consulting Special Needs Customers

Special needs groups offer special problems for those wishing to seek the views of users. By definition the users require additional care and support. This may be of a temporary nature, and the individuals may be willing and able to comment constructively on the service and demand poor service be corrected, such as residents of a women's refuge or young single homeless project.

Other groups may present a greater challenge. The users of a Care and Repair scheme are likely to both hold low expectations and be highly dependent on the scheme staff for service delivery. In such cases satisfaction surveys reveal little about the quality of the scheme.

This is even more true of high level care schemes, for the frail elderly and people with learning difficulties. In these cases a proxy for the customer may be able to offer feedback on service standards. This may be in the form of a relative, a social worker or other representative of the client, possibly the organisation paying for the care.

Some associations, like Moat and Charter HA have been working to develop charters setting out both the philosophy which underpins their special needs provision and service standards within each aspect of the service.

These outcomes however only go part way to revealing the difficulties inherent in this area, of multiple stakeholders and powerless consumers.

Multiple Stakeholders

It is clear that from both the local authority and housing association perspective, housing organisations need to attempt to satisfy multiple stakeholders. The relationship of supplier-customer does not exist in social housing.

For profit making organisations, customer satisfaction or any other stated objective, including business operation, is secondary to the financial objective. Shareholders look to the bottom line, and unless good will and quality service deliver a return, the organisation should switch strategies or its area of business operation.

In social housing, both housing associations and local authorities are bound by legislation or their own rules, to pursue social values. By definition they are about improving their district or addressing housing need. Without this mission the organisation's reason for being collapses.

The difficulty for social housing organisations comes in measuring the quality of these services, and satisfying the competing interests of numerous stakeholders. The views on quality of tenants who receive a service may differ from those who provide it, and who operate by 'professional standards'. Funders have different measures again. A building society considering a private finance loan of £5 million to an association will consider different criteria to that of the Housing Corporation, who attempt to balance financial viability against management ability and service delivery. The larger the number of groups who have an interest or influence over the organisation the more difficult the process of building these views into the service becomes.

A standard answer to overcome this conflict does not exist. However, organisations may employ a number of tactics to assist them in building a consensus on strategy or service delivery.

Firstly, acknowledgement of the multiple stakeholders is important. Who they are and what power they hold. From this point a set of priorities may be established, which, in part, reflects the organisation's own mission. A housing association needs to balance the views of existing customers seeking property improvements against assisting a partner local authority who wishes to see the association target its reserves to a new build scheme for homeless families. In this complex world, ranking priorities one to ten may be insufficient. Instead, weighting of priorities, however difficult, may provide a guide in later decision making.

Secondly, an objective should be to achieve a consensus. The Housing Investment Programme presentations which encourage all interested to be represented, enable each group to listen and understand opposing views or priorities. If pre-presentation discussion takes place within a similar forum, the housing strategist can seek a consensus on priorities for investment. In a different context, tenant federation meetings with representatives from different estates may allow the housing contractor to identify a consensus on service delivery standards.

Finally, the objective of the organisation should be to mix both short and long term demands. While the Department of the Environment may want a clearly defined long term strategy, tenants' preferences may indicate short term and responsive priorities. While expressed formally in this way, both groups are likely to want both outcomes, long and short term. The Department of the Environment expects flexibility and entrepreneurship in responding to announcements of additional funding and tenants expect a plan to improve homes and provide new housing for sons and daughters over successive years.

Summary

- For social housing providers there is no single dominant customer group. Social housing providers have multiple customers, with competing and opposing interests which they must serve.

- the introduction of CCT in housing services to local government and the extension of associations' role into management requires the consideration of new customer groups.

- the balancing of multiple stakeholder interests is difficult and complex, particularly if organisations are to avoid bowing to the needs of those with the greatest economic or political power

- using weighing, derived from open discussions between competing stakeholders, enables actions to be prioritised in an environment with limited resources.

CHAPTER 7:
GETTING CLOSE TO
CUSTOMERS

Introduction

In this chapter we will:

- look in detail at how the best at customer service go about the task of finding out what their customers expect.

- explain the importance of understanding the gap between perception and expectation of service and how that gap comes about.

- explain the fundamental importance of knowing your customers by becoming obsessed with listening to them.

- propose a model approach to getting close to the customer. This model explains the value of segmentation, expectation analysis, conditioning customers and benchmarking the best. It also sets out the relative value of such techniques as large scale satisfaction surveys, focus groups, service experience surveys and behavioural studies.

The Gap Between Expectation and Perception of Service

Customer service is now recognised by private and public organisations alike not only as highly desirable, but as a key business strategy.

We have looked at why this has become so important and at broad management strategies to help deliver good customer service. We want to look in more detail at the kinds of processes and techniques that can be used to bring about changes in management attitudes and skills so that an organisation can focus itself on satisfying its customers. We draw freely on the experiences of both the manufacturing and service sectors and the private and public sector. We also provide examples of good practice from social housing agencies and we draw on these experiences to propose model approaches.

The best providers of customer service have a very simple view of what produces satisfied customers. It is when the customers' perception of the service delivered is better than their expectations; in effect you surprise the customer. Empirical American research by V.A. Zeithamel, A Parasuraman and L.L. Berry has come up with a useful definition – service gap. Service gap is the extent to which customer perception of performance falls short of customer expectations. The customer is dissatisfied when perceptions fall short of expectation, they pass on their bad experiences and so the reputation of the service provider falls. The repairs reputation of many social housing agencies has suffered enormously from this perception of poor service.

Figure 1 – Service Gaps

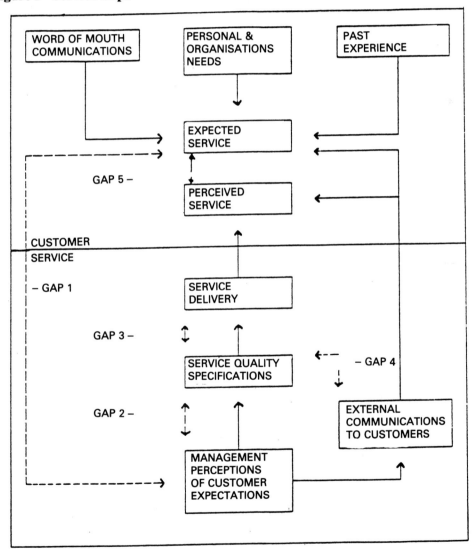

In figure one, is a representation of the service gaps which emerged from the research of Zeithamel, Parasuraman and Berry. In the customer's domain is the gap between expected service and perceived service (Gap 5). Expectations develop from needs, word of mouth and previous experience of service provided and what the organisation says it will do. Perceptions are customer opinions of the service provider as a result of experiencing the service.

According to research findings Gap 1 is the biggest underlying cause of customer dissatisfaction. Managers have incorrect views of customer needs and expectations. The next biggest gap is Gap 4 in which the wrong external signals are communicated – for example promises are made which cannot be met. Gap 2 occurs when misleading signals get to staff about tasks and standards; and gap 3 occurs when actual service does not meet specifications laid down.

Knowing the mechanisms that cause the gaps allows managers to introduce processes for improving service by closing the service gaps and keeping them closed. In this and the next chapter we will look at how the private sector has responded to the customer service challenge and whether social landlords would benefit by responding in similar ways.

The first and most important lesson to learn from those who excel at customer service is that they are obsessed with listening to their customers. They have developed a raft of techniques to ensure they understand what their customers expect, and from this they can design services and an approach to service which surprises them with its quality.

There are social housing agencies who have adopted some of these techniques and examples are given. However, housing associations and local authorities do not exploit the full range of techniques that can be used to gain awareness of customer needs and expectations.

The Importance of Knowing Your Customers

Any customer service strategy must start with an understanding of the market in which the organisation wants to operate. Who are the customers? What are their expectations needs and desires? What are their social habits their income and their freedom to exercise choice? The major obstacle to meeting customer expectations in Zeithamel, Berry and Parasuraman's gap analysis is the gap between management's perception of customer needs and expectations and the customers actual needs and expectations. Where an organisation defines its service standards based on the former, there is a good chance customers expectations will not be met. To avoid this mistake and close this gap, an organisation has to put in place processes to enable them to understand expectations and changes in expectations. They must then deliver to those expectations and ensure their communication on their services matches their performance.

In the competitive world of the private service and industrial sector, the customer responds quickly to the failure to understand and meet expectations by going to another supplier who does. Companies wishing to increase their market share do so by improving their intelligence about the customers they want to capture. The best at customer service are companies who have become obsessed with listening; who give equal status to feedback from customers in their organisations performance information; and who put in place a variety of structured techniques to get the right kind of information about their customers and their customers needs and expectations.

Social housing agencies are beginning to find out more about what their customers want, but as yet they are not as sophisticated in their approach as the best service providers in the private sector. In fact, we would go so far as to say, they are backward in this. There are many reasons for this. Perhaps most important social landlords have a captive market. With nowhere else to go the customers of local authorities and housing associations will tolerate a wide variety of standards and there is little competitive pressure to find out more about the market in which the services are offered. However, with more opportunity for choice arising from such initiatives as stock transfer and compulsive competitive tendering, tenants may not always be such a captive market. Local authorities and housing associations could be at risk from private companies who put the effort into getting to know the market, to understanding expectations and to delivering to those expectations at a lower cost.

Another factor which has tended to limit the imagination of social housing agencies is their approach to customer feedback and their predisposition to take their lead from government agencies. As Bob Line housing officer with Oadby and Wigston District Council, perceptively noted:

> "Top down abstract standards from the citizens charter, Housing Corporation, Institute of Housing or whoever, carry with them a danger of pushing those managing housing to produce turgid and unresponsive organisational forms and cultures". (Line, 1992)

It is precisely because, government agencies have taken the lead in standard setting, that many housing agencies have eschewed close and continuous dialogue with their customers on the grounds that government either knows best or, even if they do not know best, they control the finance so the landlord better dance to their tune. This is a recipe for failure in establishing an effective service strategy which responds to the customer. Government agencies and even bodies like the National Federation of Housing Associations and Institute of Housing can only ever have a very general view about what customers want and this view is often determined by issues relating to financial probity, cost and the specific political agenda of ministers. The best at customer service concentrate on the desires and expectations of their particular group of customers without those expectations being refracted through the political prism of the funders and reduced to a limiting common denominator. In the last five years, government agencies have been promoting the importance of dialogue with customers. The somewhat toothless 'Citizens Charter' includes in 'The Principles of Public Service' the importance of "... regular and systematic consultation with those who use services..." and this is one of the criteria in the 'Charter Mark Award Scheme' for excellence in delivering public services. For housing associations the more tigerish 'Housing Corporation Performance Expectations' promotes a similar approach. In their 'Performance Audit Visit Manual' the Housing Corporation looks for "... regular and systematic feedback about existing services...". However, these agencies have, as yet, published little sophisticated guidance on how this might be done. In fact the experience of a number of housing associations is that the Housing Corporation is rather one dimensional in their approach to this aspect of their audit. The particular recommendation of the audit visit manual is for "... general or specific tenant satisfaction surveys" as the primary mechanism for obtaining customer feedback. Local Authorities are not subject to "you must do it this way" advice. However as recently as 1993 the Department of the Environment published a guide entitled 'Tenant Feedback : A Step-by-Step Guide to Tenant Satisfaction Surveys'. This guide was a comprehensive document within the narrow brief of how to carry out a quantifiable satisfaction survey, but it begs the question as to whether satisfaction surveys of this type are, on their own, a useful mechanism for getting to know what customers want.

Finally there is a tradition within housing that there is a particular way of doing things, dominated by a rent collection approach to housing management, which is rarely challenged. Associated with it is a perception of the role of housing management as being beyond accountability. Housing managers often think of themselves as the last resort – the all purpose social service agency. Even to discuss private sector techniques in this context may be seen as a threat because it will lead to a product centred rather than a people centred approach. 'Private sector' approaches are now fashionable amongst those trying to change public sector management and the entrenched practitioners in a public sector like social housing see them at best as inappropriate and at worse a threat to 'a needs based' social service. Private sector techniques, the argument goes, are rooted in a search for market share in a competitive arena while social housing is concerned with the allocation of scarce resources to a deserving poor and the pursuit of better service will raise expectations that cannot be met.

These arguments are rooted in a traditional paternalistic approach to housing management which is being challenged in other ways, notably through the drive for greater tenant participation in housing management. This participation initiative tends to be driven by sacrosanct concepts of political accountability in the management of public resources. Such an assumption is alien in other service sectors even where government has provided funds in the form of grants or as shareholders. The argument in these pages is that political accountability and participation in management is a secondary issue. The primary issue is that tenants are customers of a service who, for their rent, want the very best service that can be delivered. The private service sector has adopted a quality and value for money stance to preserve market share. The means they have used can reasonably be investigated by social landlords to deliver the same quality and value for money, albeit with the idea of human justice just slightly ahead of market share on the agenda of ends. So let us now turn to some characteristics of the approach adopted by those that excel in customer service.

Getting Close to the Customer – A Model Approach

There is a revealing story about how Toyota went about producing an executive car for the United States market to challenge the pre-eminence of Mercedes, General Motors and Jaguar. They used statistical market research techniques and competitor analysis but in addition they sent a team of designers to live in an affluent American community that comprised a good cross section of the type of customers they wanted to capture. They wanted those who were designing the car to establish an empathy with those customers – what were their values, how did they live – and relate this to their expectation of the cars they wanted. The result was the Toyota Lexus which very quickly built up a substantial market share in one of the most conservative groups of the car buying public. The driving force of this approach is revealing. Toyota had a clear idea of the market in which they wanted to operate; they were able to analyze the characteristics of that market; they knew in great detail what their competitors were providing and found out how well it was viewed; and perhaps most important, they found out about the attitudes of their customers by living alongside them.

This holistic approach to finding out about customers is increasingly widespread in the private service sector. All kinds of techniques have been adopted from statistical analysis of satisfaction to complex behavioural analysis of customers and staff at the 'moment of truth' when they interact at the delivery of a service. There is a whole library of books and articles on the best ways to get to know your customers, and it is impossible to give a comprehensive survey of the myriad of approaches. However, in general to become a master of customer service you need to adopt a research strategy with four main dimensions.

The 4 Dimensions of a Research Strategy

1. *Customer Segmentation*   They will analyze their actual and potential customer base in detail, segment them and then vary their products and services to suit the different segments.

2. *Expectation Analysis*   Whilst they will develop mechanism to measure customer satisfaction with existing services, they will put more emphasis on expectation analysis and try and answer such questions as

---

what do customers expect from a product and service, and how can they keep track of changing expectations?

3. *Conditioning* They will attempt to bring customer expectations into line with the limits of their service strategy.

4. *Benchmarking* They will continually track the services of their competitors and try and ensure their services are better than those of their competitors or fill a gap in the market that their competitors have missed.

Social housing agencies need to adopt an approach to customer analysis which incorporates these elements if they are to stand alongside the masters of customer service. Let us now turn to each of these elements, analyze them in more detail, give some examples of how the techniques have been applied and point to ways in which they are or might be applied by social housing agencies.

Customer Segmentation

Segmentation in General

In his 'Managing in the Service Economy' James Heskett noted when discussing services in general that:

> "A service cannot be all things to all people. Unlike product manufacturers, service organisations can have considerable difficulty delivering more than one 'product', more than one type or level of service at one time. Groups or 'segments' of customers must be singled out for a particular service, their needs determined and a service concept developed... Segmentation is the process of identifying groups of customers with enough characteristics in common to make possible the design and presentation of a product or service each group needs". (Heskett, 1986 pp 8–9)

A sophisticated understanding of the requirements of different segments of customers is an essential part of most successful customer service strategies. A big hotel chain like Trust House Forte have a variety of hotel styles to suit different customers or the same customers who require a different type of service at different times. To take two examples. There is the large hotel catering for conference visitors, ordinary business people, foreign tourists and families on holiday. The emphasis is on a highly personal customer service which means lots of flexible warm human interaction and a wide range of facilities and services. In addition, Trust House Forte have identified a distinct customer segment who require a more basic service. These are travellers needing a comfortable, low cost overnight stopover. The solution was the Travel Lodge. They are built by motorways and trunk roads. Access to them all is controlled by a central telephone desk. The rooms replicate the facilities in most standard hotels and can meet the needs of single people, couples and families. The service is a low-touch do-it-yourself approach for speed, efficiency and low cost. What Trust House Forte did was segment their customers. With a clear understanding of the habits, expectations and attitudes of the long distance traveller they are able to provide an appropriate service.

Social landlords have carried out some high level segmentation. The most obvious example is the differentiation of services provided to retired people. Most social landlords work across the full range of housing. They provide specialist housing for retired people comprising specific types of homes, the sheltered housing scheme. They also provide specific services, warden support, alarm systems, social activities and so on. Within this specific market further segmentation has happened with the development of initiatives such as care and repair and schemes for the frail elderly. A simiiar process has developed in respect of other kinds of special needs housing where care is an integral part of the overall provision. Other examples of segmentation by the housing sector based on a more sophisticated understanding of the market in which they work includes the introduction of translation services for customers whose first language is not English, and the attempt to design homes which can be adapted to suit the different lifestyles of groups who have different cultural and religious practices.

However, sophisticated segmentation is not a common practice amongst social landlords. By and large variations to core housing management services are few and they are delivered in the same way to all tenants. Where there is variation it usually comes in the form of bolt on supplementary care packages. A typical core service is the repairs service. Most landlords have differentiated this service in accordance with criteria based on urgency of repair. Urgency is determined by considerations such as health and safety, potential or actual structural damage, or the fact that a fault is not a major inconvenience and so does not require immediate attention. This is sound practice and at a basic level is a response to tenant expectations. However, over and above this differentiation, few landlords have developed variations to this service based on the segmentation of their tenants by lifestyle or attitude. If this was taken into account, the customer service strategy in respect of repairs might be further developed. Thus, the tenant who is willing and able to help produce the service for themselves by doing repairs may only need a manual or telephone access to a help service. The tenant who is unable or unwilling to do any repairs and is at home most of the working day can be flexible in their availability to receive the service. The personal contact may also be as important a part of the service as the carrying out of the repair. Elderly tenants typically fall into this category. In contrast, some tenants may prefer a low-touch service. For example a working couple or individual who may want a flexible and quick reporting system and reliable appointment based service often outside normal office hours. Customer segmentation is an essential pre-requisite to this kind of customer service strategy.

An Example of Segmentation in the Private Sector

In the commercial world segmentation usually results in the identification of a particular target group, the development of a service to suit that target group and the decision to let other companies provide different kinds of services to different segments. Some good examples of this approach in the service sector can be found in banking, particularly in the USA. Here there is a strong independent banking sector and pundits predicted the death of the small town bank when deregulation opened local markets to efficient regional banks. However, small banks have continued to survive and prosper by segmenting customers and focusing on certain segments the regional banks do not satisfy. University National Bank and Trust (UNBT) of Palo Alto California responded to this challenge by defining a niche in the market and delivering a specific range of services which exploited what they saw as a market opportunity. UNBT has one office, discourages small depositors by setting a high monthly fee for current cheque accounts and waives the fees only where monthly balances are kept in excess of £2000. New customers are only accepted after credit check and bouncing two cheques closes the account. UNBT continues to gain market share. It has identified a customer segment who are wealthy and serves only those customers but it offers a highly personal service with a specialized range of additional services such as free travellers cheques and streamlined approval of large loans. More important than any of these features however was, according to its chairman "… the concept that we would keep the ½ of 1% of (customers who are) bad guys out of the bank's customer base. It is that ½ of 1% that causes the large banks to create the arbitrary rules that in turn create the hassle experienced in the large bank". (Davidow et al 1989 p59)

Segmentation in Social Housing

In reality many service agencies cannot segment their customers as sharply as UNBT. The set of existing customers is too diverse to be pigeonholed. This is particularly true of social landlords. Housing managers might warm to the possibility of keeping 'the bad guys' out of their customer base, but they cannot pick and chose if they are to deliver services to the current market. Social housing agencies do not have the freedom, nor should they, to develop a favourable niche in their diverse market. However, housing managers would also recognise that many of their highly bureaucratic processes which influence services to every tenant are often determined by the needs of a very small minority who are actual or potential 'bad guys'. Yet there is little external pressure to change. At a very basic level lack of variation and subtlety in the delivery of services to enhance customer satisfaction does not matter so much when the customer finds it difficult, if not impossible, to find a new supplier who does. However, it is important to recognise that the customer base of a housing association or a local authority – both in terms of applicants for homes and occupiers – is very diverse, even within the common denominator of low income households in housing need. High level segmentation is straightforward –

families, single people, single parents, the elderly, employed/not employed, dependent on benefits, ethnic minorities and so on. But even within these categories and running across them are potentially other distinctive segments who are likely to require different things from the same services if they are to be satisfied.

The lessons from the commercial world where sophisticated segmentation can mean survival or failure is that time spent identifying a sophisticated matrix of customer segments is time well spent. It allows and encourages service development which can have enormous benefits for customer satisfaction and productivity. Simply put, it enables an organisation to chose the best mix and level of service for different customer segments. Provide too little service of the wrong kind and customers will be dissatisfied, provide too much even of the right kind and costs will be higher than they need to be.

Segmentation, is not easy to do. Segmentation based on social, economic or family structure patterns may not correlate with segmentation based on attitudes such as a preference for low-touch non-personalised service or high-touch personal services. The elderly are assumed to like high-touch services, are unhappy with self-service practices such as automatic cash dispensers or payment machines, whereas economically active, young people are impatient of slow personal service and are willing to contribute to service delivery by using 'high-tech' facilities. This kind of correlation needs to be proved rather than assumed before a segmentation strategy is developed and linked to service types and levels.

In one respect social landlords are in a good position to carve out different customer segments. In order to select a tenant and allocate a home a wide range of information about household structure and circumstances is obtained. The customer base is easy to get at to obtain more information since they are in a known geographical area. The information on census returns is relatively easy to use again because it is geographically sorted and often meshes with the geography of a landlord's customer base. In addition social landlords also have access to all the other social trend research used extensively by the private sector. Indeed, there is a small industry devoted to the lifestyles, economic power and even attitudes of different socio-economic groups. The social housing sector has a small part of this industry devoted to its clients. Organisations like the Joseph Rowntree Memorial Trust provide a steady stream of research studies on different aspects of social housing including analysis of the different customer segments who are serviced by housing association and local authorities. Universities in Birmingham, Glasgow, Salford and Cardiff, to name but a few, produce a range of studies either directly or working through government departments and professional bodies. The problem is sifting the information and trying to focus it on the issue of different customer segments and their expectation of services. In particular what is missing is the correlation of a particular identifiable social economic or household type with a particular set of attitudes about what services are important and how they should be delivered. There is probably no short cut for landlords to the task of carrying out their own studies on how they should segment their customers and design and present the service each segment needs.

If this approach was adopted a landlord could develop a matrix of services which balances high cost close support services for some tenants with a much lower cost and more arms length service for others without reducing customer satisfaction. Most housing management services have evolved on the basis of a housing officer with a patch of tenancies. The size of each patch being determined by the needs of a minority of tenants who are a problem or who require close support. Segmentation could provide a methodology for challenging some of the basic organisation and service assumptions and in so doing suggest new approaches which could reduce costs, hold down rents but still meet the expectations of each segment.

An Example of Segmentation in Social Housing

Let us finish this discussion with a particular example from a midlands housing association where a particular service was developed and varied following an exercise in finding out what different segments of their tenants wanted. One of the services available was debt counselling and money advice. A service specification was developed for a particular segment of customers. This service was developed following a programme of help for tenants on claiming their full entitlement to welfare benefits. Having helped tenants with benefit, it became apparent that many tenants having received their full entitlement were still finding it difficult to meet their housing costs. Initially a service specification was developed for two particular segments of customers. First, those on low incomes, usually with arrears of rent and who had received all their benefit entitlement but still could not manage their housing costs within their income. Second the elderly who were on fixed incomes and, though not in arrears, had a fear of falling into arrears. In both cases the service requirement was for a highly personal, high-touch service based on intensive individual counselling. It is a costly service to deliver, but the productivity gains achieved in reducing rent arrears and the associated sense of a service which focused on a help culture rather than policing culture, justified the cost.

When the association assessed the value to customers of this service through a series of focus groups, they further identified another segment of customers who expressed an interest in such a service and were unaware that the association could offer such a service. However, this segment of customers was much broader and though on low incomes were not such a high risk in terms of arrears. What they wanted was not a high-touch and, consequently, costly individual counselling service but more of a simple self-help service. The association therefore developed a free financial advice and debt management booklet. It was developed in consultation with this segment of customers and provided them with a simple step by step guide to personal financial management and how to deal with debt. It was low-touch, did not require the customer to disclose personal information about which they were embarrassed, and gave them the freedom to use the service when they wanted, and without waiting for some inconvenient personal counselling session.

This example of segmentation came about by accident rather than through a sophisticated analysis of the customer base. However, it brought home the lesson that services need to be varied for different groups of customers. It showed that an effective customer service strategy means finding out who your customers are and what they expect. Segmentation takes care of the first requirement, research into expectation and satisfaction takes care of the second.

Expectation Analysis:

The Do's and Dont's

The second lesson to be learnt from the masters of customer service is that they use a variety of techniques to find out what their different customer segments want. They concentrate less on a historical view of satisfaction and more on the expectations of customers. Pinpointing customers' expectations is not always easy, particularly in a service like social housing. Housing associations and local authorities actually provide two products, a home and a housing management service. To find out about customers expectations of a home is the easy part. The product is tangible and you can focus on key elements such as size, location, fittings and fixtures, and heating performance. Having found out what the customers expect and conditioned them to what can be delivered within the limitations imposed by cost of provision and amount of rent they are likely to have to pay, it is relatively straightforward to ensure the home meets expectation, before they actually experience the product. It can be checked to ensure it conforms to the specification and that it is fit for purpose. It is much more difficult to research customer expectation of the housing management service. Services include hard, easily measurable quantities like speed of repair, time taken to process a benefit claim and accuracy of rent accounts, and soft elusive qualities like feelings of being respected and listened to. In the last resort service can never be inspected before actual delivery. The process guiding a service can be measured for reliability, conformity and timeliness, but unlike the home or the process, the actual service involves simultaneous production and consumption. The nature of expectation of service is inexorably tied up with who performs the service. William Davidow and Bro Uttal in their 'Total Customer Service' emphasise that research into what customers expect of a service:

> ".... is stymied because services are intangible; because they are hard to standardize; because customers judgements of service are coloured by who performs the service and by their own involvement in producing it, and because a service is hard to distinguish from the manner in which it's produced and delivered". (Davidow et al 1989 p 71)

But the key message from the gurus of customer service is that research, however difficult, pays off. The methods of research need to be varied. The aim is to become obsessed with listening and find all sorts of ways to listen and to keep listening. In adopting a sophisticated approach to such research, five key do's and don'ts need to be addressed.

*   **Don't assume you know what customers expect.**

It is common for social housing agencies to be very inward looking when it comes to deciding what their customers want and they are easily guided by industry norms, usually enshrined in government circulars, and their own past practices. Housing managers, like all professional groups pump up their own expertise. The comments of Karl Albrecht and Ron Zemke in their 'Service America', will strike a chord with housing professionals.

> "There is often a great deal of assuming or guessing going on in service organizations about the customers' attitudes and habits. It is common for those who run service organizations to form their views of the customer through long years of experience but with little actual data. Each manager has a theory about what is important to the customer, but in relatively few cases is this theory actually grounded in reasonably sophisticated research". (Albrecht et at 1985 p 59)

In housing, staff who determine customer service strategy are usually those whose daily routine is taken up with the problems of a minority of tenants. For the majority of tenants service contact can be infrequent and short. Moreover it is more likely to be with a contractor, a receptionist or someone dealing with a rent payment. These are the 'moments of truth' that define the attitude and perception of most customers to the organisation.

*   **Don't rely exclusively on the all service satisfaction survey.**

General satisfaction surveys measure the past, whereas a dynamic customer service strategy needs to focus on expectations of customers. There is also a tendency for people to express general satisfaction with a service in such surveys even though their expectations are different and often more demanding. Such surveys can generate apparent high levels of general satisfaction which can mislead or be used by managers to gloss over real service weaknesses. In a recent newsletter from a regional office of the National Federation of Housing Associations a housing association reported that 80% of its tenants ranked its services good to excellent and if those ranking the service as acceptable were included the scores ".... soar...." to over 90%. This kind of analysis and attitude appears frequently in the housing press. Looked at another way, then up to 20% of these tenants did not have their expectations met, so, in a stock of 5,000, 1,000 tenants could be unhappy and in a stock of 10,000, 2,000 could be unhappy – a lot of people. In the private service sector this would mean a potential market erosion to competitors of 20%. A recipe for commercial disaster. Satisfaction surveys are frequently conceived by staff brainstorming a list of service attributes, turning them into a questionnaire, administering the questionnaire to hundreds of customers and precisely tabulating the answers. As in the example above, the result is often a persuasive argument for adopting a service strategy that maintains the virtues and vices of the existing strategy.

Large market research exercises generate highly accurate but potentially misleading numbers. The people usually motivated to fill in voluntary postal surveys are the extremely satisfied and the extremely dissatisfied. Whilst random sampling can throw up groups of customers who, although representing a fairer cross section of the customer base, nonetheless may be asked to give opinions on some services of which they have had no recent experience.

As we note below, satisfaction surveys have their place, but they have fundamental weaknesses if used as the only or main mechanism for getting close to the customer.

* **Do go for open ended questions, focus groups and other non-directive research methods.**

Since pinpointing customer expectations is most important in developing a customer service strategy, then inevitably the questions to be asked need to be open ended. Such an approach is not easily done through typical 'closed question' survey techniques. Instead, the supplier of the service needs to enter into a dialogue with its customers. This is particularly the case when it comes to the way services are delivered, the degree to which different customer segments want to contribute to service provision through self-help techniques or alternatively want a 'high-touch' personal service.

The relative value of different kinds of service is also best ascertained through these open ended research techniques. One of the most famous examples of how this approach influenced a service strategy is British Airways. When British Airways wanted to transform itself into the service leader, it asked incoming passengers open ended questions about what they expected of an airline. Four qualities came out as most important – two expected and two a surprise. The expected qualities were the care and concern demonstrated by staff on the airplanes and in the airport, and the ability of front line employees to solve problems. The two unexpected qualities were the need for staff to show spontaneity and flexibility in applying company policies and the ability to recover from mistakes by making things right for the passenger. (Bruce, 1987)

To get at expectations through open ended questions tends to promote a research methodology which puts the emphasis on small focus groups of customers and front line employees who can debate the nature of the existing service and where service falls below, or exceeds expectations. This can then be followed up with more detailed research which can be targeted to particular services or particular customer segments.

* **Do concentrate on service experience surveys.**

The all service satisfaction survey with its random sampling can become little more than a popularity poll that measures the general perception of the overall service, without tying together the views of those who have recently experienced a service and the survey. A better alternative is to adopt the technique of following up on recent transactions. Limiting customer surveys to those customers with recent service experience ensures you are measuring service performance not general perception. This is easily done in social housing since it is relatively straightforward to track those tenants who have come into contact with their landlord for one service or another.

This approach also enables the introduction of a process of continuous and frequent measurement. The large scale popularity poll approach of all service satisfaction surveys can be expensive and time consuming to organise. This inevitably means they are usually done infrequently. In contrast service experience surveys are much more powerful tools. They can be more easily integrated into routine procedures as the final step in the procedure. They can be done frequently and on a small scale which is much more sharply focused. They can be carried out directly by the front line staff providing the service, thus making listening to the customer an integral and immediate part of their job. Such continuous measurement means the landlord can track changing expectations more quickly and develop services which are much more flexible to a rapidly changing service environment.

* **Do Integrate Customer Expectations into the Organizations Performance Measures**

Most organisations have introduced measures for controlling the quality of customer service. Mostly these measures are process or product measures. In housing the process measures include such things as how long it takes to do a repair, how quickly an application for housing is processed, how long it takes to resolve a complaint, how quickly a void property is relet. Product measures relate to the quality of the house or flat, such as its state of repair, its size, facilities available in the home and its heating performance. The performance indicators required by regulatory bodies and set out in guidance manuals such as the National Federation of Housing Associations' 'Improving your Use of Performance Indicators' concentrate on these kinds of measures. Such measures are necessary but they can be dangerous in the context of a customer service strategy if they are unrelated to customer expectations. The problem with them is that the measures tend to focus on averages. By selecting averages, managers recognise that variability is inevitable in service delivery. But averages can accommodate enormous extremes. If the standard of completing all non-urgent repairs within 3 weeks is relevant in that this is what customers expect, an average of 3 weeks can include many repairs completed in one week which incurs costs with no increase in customer satisfaction; as well as repairs which take longer than 3 weeks with the result that customers become annoyed and are quick to tell other people about the poor quality of the service. If the landlord only focuses its measurement system on such product and process measures, employees will tend to do exactly what the measures tell them to do. What is needed is a set of customer expectations and satisfaction measures to go alongside these product and process measures. Continual feedback from customers is the only answer. The best in customer service make customer expectation and satisfaction measures an integral part of the measurement system. Such feedback is used to test the validity of the process measures so that when a discrepancy occurs, the managers know it is time to change the process measures. It is no good targeting a monthly turnround on repairs when tenants expect a two week turnround.

Ways of Understanding Expectations

We know of no social landlord that has developed an approach to understanding customer expectations which incorporates all these various do's and don'ts. However, increasingly social landlords are becoming aware of some of these techniques and are experimenting with them. Set out below is a possible model drawing on examples of various practices adopted by different social landlords which, if combined would make up a strong and effective research strategy to enable a landlord to find out what customers expect. The model has four elements:

* focus groups
* complaints & general satisfaction surveys
* service experience surveys
* monitoring customer care

Focus Groups

The keystone of our customer research model is focus groups. These are a particularly powerful tool in getting much closer to customer expectations, because of their flexibility and ability to employ open ended questions. Focus groups can be geared to a particular customer segment and their expectations; they can be geared to a particular service being offered; they can be geared to the way staff handle 'moments of truth' in respect of any service; they can be set up on a continuous basis through a panel or number of panels of tenants whose membership changes on a particular cycle; or they can be one off exercises with groups of tenants. The methodology can vary to include questionnaires of closed questions and more open ended debates where customers can build on the ideas of others. Their membership can be a mixture of front line staff and customers, or just customers. They can be run by the landlord or by an outside consultant or facilitator. Normally they would involve at least 8 and probably no more than 16 participants. If the landlord wants the views of a wide group of people then more focus groups should be set up, rather than make each focus group bigger. The focus groups may need to be drawn from different geographical areas or from tenants or applicants who deal with different offices or different housing officers. The membership of any group will vary depending upon the purpose. In some cases openness may require an approach where representatives of the landlord are not present and an outside facilitator controls the proceedings. In other cases, where it is appropriate for the discussion to include comments or information about the constraints on a landlord to deliver particular levels of service, then the presence of a representative of the landlord can be beneficial.

Whatever the membership, simply sitting around a table with customer representatives will not necessarily shed light on problems and expectations. The structure of the meeting needs to be considered so it does not end up as a talking shop. Topics for discussion must be specified. For example, the group might be concentrating on one particular area of service rather than all services. Also tools such as brainstorming or Pareto Analysis may to be used to help people open up, develop ideas and assess their significance in terms of customer service. This itself might require training for these groups in these techniques. Whatever the techniques, the primary purpose of most focus groups should be to identify what is important to the customer, clearly establish expectations, find out how good the customer thinks the landlord is at providing it and building a specification for the service that the customer is happy with.

The use of focus groups in this way is becoming more widespread amongst social housing agencies, but they are not as widely used as traditional satisfaction surveys. Where they have been used, the impetus has not usually been the development of a sophisticated view about understanding and improving customer service, but rather as a by-product of the pressure being applied to housing associations and local authorities to develop tenant participation policies.

Using Focus Groups in Social Housing

This is what happened at the Leicester Housing Association where they have introduced consumer advisory panels. In the words of David Saviour, the Chief Executive

"In a search for a viable concept and methodology for tenant participation Leicester Housing Association started from the premise that most current models of tenant participation were outmoded in terms of the present consumer age; that the paternalism and 'tokenism' of co-optees to management committees as a single or small number of supposedly representative people should be avoided and that any new initiative needed to be set within a broad strategy. Finally, if participation was to have a central purpose, it should be about the quality of access for consumers and the quality of service" (Seviour, 1993 p 34)

Leicester Housing Association has introduced a strict mechanism for selecting these consumer advisory panels. They trained their front line staff in involving tenants in consumer discussions. A guide book was prepared for a series of over 70 meetings involving a full range of their tenants. At these meetings a service audit exercise was carried out using a questionnaire requiring specific and open ended responses. The questionnaire focused on four issues. Leicester Housing Association as a landlord, the tenants' own accommodation and perceptions of value for money, the local area and environment, and 'one thing', 'best thing', and 'worst thing' comments. Also at these meetings the proposal for continuing consumer advisory panels was discussed, and a number of candidates came forward for two advisory panels. The candidates stood for election to the panels and on a 55% postal ballot, two advisory panels were set up.

The service audit exercise enabled the association to home in on poor services by small, localised areas and

"Equally important, it also enables future consumer advisory panel agendas to be more accurately informed about service delivery and hopefully thereby prevents participation being about endless dialogue about mythologies of performance". (Seviour, 1993 p 35)

Derby District Council adopted a similar approach forming a series of customer panels. Again, it was an approach which came out of a desire to improve tenant participation. Derby had originally tried to set up residents associations, but only 1000 of 17,250 tenants had been involved. Customer panels were seen as a way of overcoming the apathy associated with such traditional methods of consultation. A customer panel is a meeting between customers local housing staff, ward councillors and a member of the housing committee. Each panel meets every two months and there are a number of different objectives including the involvement of customers in decision making which is delegated to estate level; monitoring the performance of local housing offices; controlling delegated budgets and target resources; and identifying investment priorities and providing feedback to the housing committee.

At Coventry Churches Housing Association (CCHA) the use of focus groups was the result of dissatisfaction with the traditional survey method. Every 3 or 4 years since 1976, CCHA had carried out satisfaction surveys amongst all its tenants. However, in 1989 it was decided that a new approach should be tried which focused attention more on expectation. Initially the idea was to carry out a small scale qualitative study to provide an in depth understanding of residents needs and perceptions and to steer development of a later full scale satisfaction survey. The method adopted was to carry out a range of group discussions with different segments of CCHA's customers. The customers were segmented into tenants in general purpose housing, tenants in sheltered housing, shared ownership leaseholders in general purpose housing and shared ownership leaseholders in sheltered housing. There was also a focus group comprising front line housing management staff. The selection of participants and the discussions themselves were handled by a consultancy specialising in social and business planning and research. The participants were recruited by personal contact and simple quotas were applied to each session. Thus, such factors as the proportion of assured tenants to secure tenants was considered since assured tenants represented the future pattern of tenancy. Some of the sessions comprising elderly home owners involved recent buyers and others long-standing owners. The staff session was drawn exclusively from front line housing management staff covering both rented and home ownership properties.

Each session lasted from between 1 hour and 2 hours. Discussion was informal and all were taped and transcribed for detailed analysis. All interviews were carried out on a confidential basis. In the subsequent report liberal use was made of verbatim quotations because these gave a flavour of the way people think, talk and feel. The sessions were kept fluid around eight broad headings – perceptions of CCHA, paths to CCHA, aspirations and expectations, general satisfaction, range and quality of services, accommodation, rents and charges, and information from CCHA to occupiers. The whole purpose of this approach was to provide understanding rather than statistics and to focus on perceptions and expectations rather than just satisfaction. The resulting messages were both predictable and surprising. For example, CCHA had been developing a strategy of choice for people to move from one type of tenure to another as their circumstances changed, but few occupiers expected such a developing housing path. Much more important to occupiers was for CCHA to supply a set of core services well, to keep costs down and to act as a reasonable landlord. In respect of a particular service like repairs, the expectation, predictably enough, was for a fast response, but equally important was the desire for good information if a repair was going to be delayed or there was some difficulty in sorting out a particularly stubborn repair. The personal nature of the way services were delivered was welcomed, but again occupiers wanted better communication about what personal support services were provided and by whom. It was this response that led to the introduction of different approaches to debt counselling based on personal counselling for some residents and a self-help manual for others which has been described earlier in this chapter.

Complaints & General Satisfaction Surveys

Another building block in the model is complaints analysis and satisfaction surveys. These are two mechanisms that are particularly useful tools in pinpointing major performance problems. There is now available plenty of practical guidance for housing staff in how to conduct and use satisfaction surveys. In 1985 Paddington Churches Housing Association published Arun Misra's 'A Guide to Tenant Surveys' and in 1993 the Department of the

Environment published 'Tenant Feedback: A Step-by-Step Guide to Tenant Satisfaction Surveys'. Both documents provide good step-by-step guides on the methodology, design, fieldwork and the processing of data and so little needs to be said here about conducting such surveys. There is also plenty of practical experience amongst social landlords since such satisfaction surveys are increasingly becoming a normal routine in housing associations and local authorities. Complaints can also be a useful guide to performance problems. The National Federation of Housing Associations published a guide called 'Dealing with complaints and compensation' in 1993. Peter Davey, its author, not only deals with the way complaints should be handled but also how they can be monitored to provide useful information on service failures and performance problems.

These two mechanisms however should not be at the centre of a research model. Complaints are not a particularly strong index of satisfaction. American research has shown that customers who complain represent a tiny fraction of all dissatisfied customers. Most people do not complain because they do not think it is worth while; while others tell their problems in passing to friends and neighbours but rarely to the organisation (Goodman 1986). Customer surveys can paint a much sharper picture than complaint rates, but, as emphasised earlier in this chapter, the closed statistical nature inherent in the methodology of such surveys severely restricts their ability to identify aspects of service that different customers segments really care about. Despite these weaknesses, satisfaction surveys and complaints will help in setting the agenda for closer studies of customer expectations. If they are carried out regularly they can also provide useful indicators on whether action taken is tackling these major performance problems.

Service Experience Surveys

Much more valuable is the third building block in our customer research model follow up research based on feedback from focus groups, complaints and general satisfaction surveys. An excellent example of how these research methods can be combined is described by William Davidow and Bro Uttal and comes from American Express. To keep abreast of customer expectations America Express' Travel Related Services Operation conducts frequent focus groups followed up by hundreds of interviews to uncover what aspects of their service customers value most. This information is then used to develop surveys of customer satisfaction that are very specific and thorough. The survey forms are short – 4 pages only – and take 10 to 15 minutes to complete. They are used in postal surveys sent to some 12,000 customers a year just after they have had some contact or transaction with American Express. Every aspect of the service American Express offers is shaped by this research. When interviewed by Davidow and Uttal, Mary Anne Rasmussen, vice president for worldwide quality assurance noted "we do transaction surveys for all kinds of experiences, not just card replacement... we hope that they (customers) feel like members of a club, that they have been treated with courtesy and respect ... whatever they talk with us about, we want them to feel better about American Express than they did before picking up the phone". (Davidow et al 1989 pp 76-77)

The significant feature about this follow up research is that it is service specific, continuous and directed at customers who have had a recent experience of a service or contact with the supplier. When CCHA carried out its study using focus groups, the intention was to follow up with a more detailed satisfaction survey focusing on the issues raised by these focus groups. Upon completion of the study, this second stage was abandoned. Instead, the emphasis was switched to a combined approach of small scale surveys of particular services amongst those who have just experienced the service, and a process of continuous survey for other services. For example, as part of the process of void control and re-letting a survey was carried out amongst those moving into re-let property about the standards they expect of those properties. This survey covered new tenants, existing tenants who were transferring and those moving as a result of mutual exchanges. One of the regional offices also carried out an expectation study on new tenants. One of the problems was the fact that when an offer was made, whilst it met general expectations in terms of size and location, it did not always meet much more heartfelt desires about decoration or specific location. The association introduced a new system to get at these specific desires and although they could not promise to meet them all, merely by focusing on them, meeting some and explaining the difficulties of meeting others, new tenants were made to feel better about CCHA than they otherwise would have done. This study, and the re-let survey were particularly valuable since they helped the association develop an approach and a style which established a positive view of the association by occupiers who were receiving their first experience of the organisation.

In addition to these small scale one off surveys, CCHA have also started to introduce a series of continuous surveys on core services experienced by most tenants. The first of these relates to the repairs service. Every repair is acknowledged in writing which gives a clear description of the repair and the date by which it will be completed. A pre-paid satisfaction card is also sent out on every repair. The card has six simple questions which were derived from feedback from the focus groups on what the groups regarded as the most important expectations of this service. The questions cover ease of reporting a repair, the friendliness and helpfulness of staff and contractors, whether the repair was completed satisfactorily, whether it was completed by the target date and whether the contractor tidied up on completion of the repair. The questions only require a simple yes or no. When the card is received back by CCHA, if any of the 'no' boxes are ticked, then staff contact the tenant to find out why there was a problem. The returned cards are analyzed every 3 months to see where the service is not meeting expectations. CCHA is not unique in adopting this

...since the survey on company cars the Chief seems to have gone off tenant consultation...

approach to finding out about tenants' views on the repairs service. The association is, however, now extending this approach to include views on the quality of re-lets by new tenants who have just moved in, and general views of service from tenants who are giving up their tenancy. This kind of approach allows the landlord to get much closer to expectations and to keep tracking them. Customer expectations do not stand still, rather there is a continuous spiral of increasing expectation. As one expectation is met it becomes established as a generic part of the service. To further develop the service and meet new expectations, the supplier must keep listening to the customer.

Monitoring Customer Care: Behavioural Studies

Satisfaction surveys and the analysis of complaints both of which highlight major service failures combined with focus groups and follow up service experience surveys, which best enable expectations to be established, are the key elements in our customer research model. They are techniques which are widely used by the masters of customer service and they readily transfer to the social housing sector. Some landlords are already employing some, if not all of these techniques, although very few have purposefully gone out to develop an all embracing model of research of the kind described here. Most of the techniques revolve around particular products or services provided by a landlord. But, as constantly emphasised by the commentators on customer service strategies, services are intangible and whatever the outputs of a particular service – repairs, statements of account, advice on benefits – a common factor in determining satisfaction is the way the service is delivered. In Jan Carlzon's phrase, this is the moment of truth when a customer interacts with a staff member or a supplier, such as a repairs contractor, working on behalf of the organisation. At the moment of truth the service is planned and delivered simultaneously; its quality cannot be inspected beforehand. Our model for a comprehensive research strategy could also usefully incorporate a fourth element, a system for monitoring customer care whatever the output service. It is a truism to say that customers want courteous, efficient and fair behaviour and that if they encounter rude and inefficient behaviour they will have a poor perception of the organisation no matter how quickly a repair is done. Customer care programmes are designed to deliver such courteous behaviour but how do you find out if these programmes work and actually deliver what customers expect. One approach is to use behavioural management techniques. Fred Luthans and others have reported how in banking, such techniques have been used successfully to identify what makes the difference in terms of exceptional customer service in the way staff react with customers. In a Midwestern bank a project was undertaken with cashiers. A group of cashiers were rated by customers immediately, but unobtrusively, following their interaction. The survey focused on the non-quantifiable nature of service using a set of dimensions such as the appearance of the staff; the expectations customers have of dependable, accurate and consistent service; the readiness and willingness of staff to serve customers promptly and efficiently making customers aware that their business is wanted and appreciated; the courtesy and competence of staff that instills confidence in customers; and the empathy of staff through individual attention and caring for the customers' needs. Within these dimensions, the study concentrated on six areas of greeting – eye contact, speed of service, degree of help offered, personal recognition of the customer, and appreciation for the customer's business.

The bank concerned already had a strong emphasis on quality service expressed through advertising and staff training. However, through the use of behavioural management techniques they were able to discover the areas that made a real difference to customer satisfaction. The procedure was to measure the perception of the quality of service received from the cashiers in terms of the dimensions described above. This was done immediately after the interaction and was carried out out of sight of the cashiers so that they were not aware that the data gathering procedure was occurring. Next, a group of cashiers were given a form of feedback called PIGS, an acronym for a behavioural management technique which stands for positive, immediate, graphic and specific. This feedback, which made this group of cashiers aware of the customer feedback, was combined with a re-enforcement procedure from supervisors who recognised and gave attention to cashiers who were observed to be the best at delivering the dimension of eye contact, speed of service, degree of help, personal recognition and appreciation. Another group of cashiers were subject to no such intervention, but were used as a control group. The study provided clear evidence of what made the difference between the customers perception of a satisfactory or good experience in their interaction with cashiers and exceptional experience and it also provided evidence of the positive impact behavioural management techniques can have on improving the delivery of quality service to bank customers. (Luthans, 1991)

We have no evidence that such a sophisticated approach to research on the moments of truth in customer service has been carried out by any social landlord.

The example of a bank from the mid west of the United States may not readily relate to a social landlord in the United Kingdom, but there are some common features which makes the comparison a useful one. Personal contact is a significant feature in the way a bank operates and in the way a social landlord delivers its services. Also, it has been widely demonstrated that, however good the product and however well designed the service, the customers' perception of an organisation is most influenced by their experience of dealing with the front line staff. Therefore behavioural studies of this kind could be effectively used in a model of customer research for housing associations and local authorities.

Through a sophisticated approach to customer segmentation and by adopting the kind of research model set out here, a landlord can find out who their customers are and what they expect. These are the two most important questions to answer before developing a workable customer service strategy. But the results may be a call for a level of service which is impossible to deliver. This is particularly a risk facing social landlords who are severely constrained by government policies and the desire to keep rents low. This leads us to the third element in the dynamics of customer service: bringing customer expectations into line with the limits of a service strategy.

Conditioning: Keeping Expectations Under Control

When a customer's expectation of a service exceeds the perceived level of service dissatisfaction is the result. When perception of the service exceeds expectation customers are surprised and in being surprised are highly satisfied. If research techniques focus on asking questions about expectation and keep asking those questions an organisation inevitably puts itself at risk of discovering expectations it can never meet and of raising awareness amongst customers of expectations that cannot be met. In these circumstances there are only 3 choices. Abandon all such research and hope that what is delivered is what is wanted. Raise the awareness but do nothing about it. Attempt to rein in expectations and try and condition customers to what is reasonable and value for money.

In one study of over 300 critical incidents in which hotel, restaurant and airline employees recalled difficult problems with customers, three quarters were due to the fact that customers' expectations were greater than could be met due to unreasonableness of the demands or the fact that they exceeded policies or cost structures. (Nugguist et al, 1985) There are many examples of this kind of problem within social housing. An obvious one is transfers. One of the core services delivered by all social landlords is the opportunity to transfer from one home to another. Any transfer policy, even a restrictive one which is based wholly on needs such as overcrowding, can rarely produce a service where a request is dealt with as quickly as the tenant expects and wants, even where need is overwhelming. Similarly the initial lettings service or major repairs and improvements to older housing stock.

The need to limit expectations on some key services is important in customer service strategies but it is not easily done. Reasonableness is a key limitation. A service performance of completing all repairs within 24 hours cannot be promised, because customers will not believe you. In the same way you cannot persuade customers that a very poor repairs service is acceptable because of problems of costs when they feel deeply that it is unreasonable. Expectations are derived from many sources including what customers believed was achieved in the past, what customers experienced from other suppliers, what friends tell them they have experienced and what publicity says can be achieved. The threshold of expectation of individual customers also varies. Education, values and experience are all different so expectations are likely to differ from one person to the next.

What is regarded as a reasonable delay by one tenant can be seen as totally unreasonable by another. However, notwithstanding such problems of reining-in expectations, the masters of customer service in the private sector do employ some effective tactics to bring expectations into line with the limits of service strategy. In particular they try and get customers to expect slightly less service than they can deliver. To do this is difficult since the aim is to contain expectations whilst trying to understand what customers really want from the service.

There is the constant danger that the organisation will try and force down expectations below the threshold that leads to alienation. Keeping the risk in mind two tactics can be employed. First, when working in focus groups or using other survey techniques it is important to suggest the limits of possibility for any service and why there are these limits. Thus, when discussing expectations of the transfer service the art is to emphasise the limited flexibility you might be able to offer despite government restrictions on building new homes and their encouragement to sell off existing homes. In the example used earlier of CCHA's focus groups this technique was carefully employed. In the focus groups the consultant readily allowed the discussions to develop into quite dramatic suggestions for improving services but always brought the groups back to the question of the possible additional cost of such service improvements and whether they would still meet expectation in respect of value for money. In general, residents felt the balance of service and cost was about right and expectations were clearly reined in to limits which were in the control of the association and which would not lead to substantially higher rents or service charges. Significantly the consumer advisory panels set up by Leicester Housing

Association and Derby's customer panels both contain or are run by staff and council members who can ensure tenants are made aware of policy, political or cost limitations on service standards and delivery.

CCHA's service experience surveys were also structured to rein in expectations. The survey on rent accounts started by listing all of the information that could be included on a rent statement based on the information on each tenancy and account held on the computer. Tenants were asked to rate the relative value of this information and add any item that was missing. Not surprisingly the list helped to define the parameters of peoples thinking and few proposed information which was not available to the association. Similarly the survey on standards of re-lets made it clear that major re-improvement of older stock to introduce new facilities was not possible within the cost constraints to which the association had to work, but thorough health and safety checks, cleaning and, in special circumstances full re-decoration, was possible. The second tactic to help rein in expectations is to use general publicity to send out messages about service. This is no more than positioning the service in the way advertisers position a product or service in the private sector. Newsletters, and meetings with residents can be used to explain how policies beyond the organisation's control limit freedom or impinge on the organisations own policies. Secondly, handbooks and leaflets explaining services can set down clear standards usually at a level slightly less than they will get. If a repair service can respond to all normal repairs in, say, two weeks, promise three.

Information about standards of performance needs to be as precise as possible. To use average performance on repairs as the basis for publicity means that the landlord is in danger of establishing an expectation threshold that some repairs will not achieve. If some repairs are going to take eight weeks, then the message has to be that most normal repairs will take, say, three weeks, but where this is not possible this will be explained and reasons for delay given. What must be avoided at all costs is the creation and widening of gap four in Zeithamel, Parasuraman and Berry's gap analysis, the market communication gap where there is a difference between what customers have been promised and what they actually experience.

The masters of customer service also use tangible clues to highlight the delivery of a service where otherwise it might not be obvious and in so doing promote a view of the supplier as an organisation doing its best within constraints. For example, if a re-let is not upgraded to the standards of a newly built home, but nonetheless is inspected for health and safety and cleanliness, leave evidence of this such as a signed checklist of work done or an obvious fresh smell and sparkle to sanitary fittings. When the Automobile Association inspect a second hand car for a potential purchaser the long checklist meticulously prepared is an important sign of the service and its thoroughness. Hotels frequently wrap tape round toilet seats to let guests know the toilet has been cleaned.

Expectations are also conditioned by experiences of other suppliers and an effective market research strategy needs to encompass research into the customer services of other organisations and how these rate in meeting expectations. This brings us to benchmarking, the last of our four main dimensions in the dynamics of understanding customer expectations.

Benchmarking: Learning From Others

Benchmarking is a technique used to identify the critical competencies that differentiate a company from its competition. A clear, if wordy, definition is "... a continuous process of measuring a company's products or services against direct competitors or those who are accepted as leaders with specific functional expertise". (Asher 1989, p 95) Its role in helping an organisation develop a customer service strategy and, specifically its role in understanding and controlling customer expectations is twofold. First, customers often set and define their expectations by reference to their best experiences of other organisations. Expectation analysis can be enormously enhanced by finding out what other organisations do that appear to meet or exceed their customers' expectations. Secondly benchmarking helps to establish the threshold of expectations and so can contribute to the task of reining in expectations. It is of little benefit for an organisation to be miles ahead of the competition when you may gain little extra in customer satisfaction but at a much greater cost. Although, of course to remain only just a little better than the best, creates the risk of easily being overtaken, and so requires a constant process of benchmarking to ensure a company does not fall too far behind the best.

Benchmarking is now widely used in the private sector. The Department of Trade and Industry, as part of its Enterprise Initiative, has published a guide called 'Best Practice Benchmarking'. This document gives advice on how to go about benchmarking and cites a handful of useful case studies. Among these is the ubiquitous example of British Airways. As part of its programme of listening to the customer to find out about and better meet expectations it has introduced a systematic programme of benchmarking. The airline recognised that one of the best ways to get at expectations was to examine in detail what other airlines believe provided them with an edge in meeting customer expectations, and conversely what they found did not meet customer expectations. They also asked their customers to compare service experiences of different airlines to establish what customers liked best. In British Airways, staff from a headquarters department are charged with providing to the board each month a detailed analysis of a different competitor not just in terms of financial information, but in terms of the services provided and how well they are received.

Rank Xerox is another company that has developed a highly sophisticated approach to benchmarking. In particular, Rank Xerox has been a pioneer of the approach of benchmarking specific functions in a variety of companies who are nothing to do with photo-copying but who nonetheless provide similar service functions. For example, John Welch, their Quality Manager has described how they

> "...compared our distribution against 3M in Dusseldorf, Ford in Cologne, Sainsbury's regional depot in Herts, Volvo's parts' distribution warehouse in Gothenburg and IBM's international warehouse and French warehouse." (Trade and Industry, Department 1989)

Social housing organisations are in one respect well placed and in another, poorly placed to exploit benchmarking as part of a process of getting close to the customer. They are well placed in that, they are not a particularly competitive service sector. Consequently it is relatively easy to establish a dialogue with other housing agencies on their services and what seems to score with customers. Also, the trade organisations produce a wide range of material on best practices. This openness, however, may soon by a thing of the past as compulsory competitive tendering develops. In another respect, social housing agencies are poorly placed to exploit benchmarking. Regular airline passengers or hotel customers will almost certainly have experience of several different suppliers and this experience can be readily tapped in the search for an understanding of customer expectations. Most customers of social landlords have limited experience of other suppliers. They have often not been free to chose a landlord, and once housed cannot easily change to another provider.

Notwithstanding these difficulties, a number of tactics can be adopted to use the experience of an applicants and tenants' contacts with other organisations to help in understanding their expectations. Some tenants who have been nominated by local authorities or who have become tenants by mutual exchange can form particular focus groups from which information can be obtained on what was good or bad about their previous landlord and how services compare. Applicants going through the process of finding a home are likely to be making application to several different landlords and so their experience of and expectations of other application processes can be obtained. Many services provided by housing associations and local authorities are broadly similar to services provided by non-housing agencies. Repairs services can be compared to similar services offered on white goods or cars. Processing a claim for housing benefit can be compared to processing a DSS claim. Reception services and the way face to face interaction on service is handled can be benchmarked against almost any company. When a tenant has only the experience of one housing association or local authority's rent payment and rent accounting service, their awareness of what could be expected will be strictly limited. But if in the dialogue with such a tenant, the comparison is drawn with similar services they have experienced from a bank, building society, post office or the electricity gas and water companies, then much higher expectations could emerge. Even in the case of tenants with the experience of several landlords, such comparisons with non-housing agencies still remains valid and useful to the understanding of expectations.

Customer requirements can only be met if both provider and customer have the same expectation of what is required. In gap analysis the biggest underlying cause of customer dissatisfaction is the information gap between management perceptions of consumer expectations and the consumer's actual expectations. The gap can only be closed if the provider has information about customer expectations. The masters of customer service in the private sector have developed a wide range of techniques to find out about their customers expectations. Most of these techniques can readily be adopted by social landlords and indeed there are some good examples of where these have been successfully applied. But few social landlords have developed the kind of sophisticated market research strategy used in service companies like British Airways or American Express. Social housing tenants cannot easily move from one supplier to another, so the incentive of competition and even survival has not driven social landlords to develop such strategies. This may change in the new and changing world of social housing, and anyway to do the best for customers by giving them a service which exceeds their expectations should be incentive enough.

Summary

To be the best at listening and to become obsessed with listening a landlord needs to adopt a customer research strategy with four key elements.

- **Customer Segmentation.**   Identify the different segments amongst the broad tenant population. Focus on the different expectation of each segment, both in terms of the actual service functions they require and whether they want low touch or high touch service. Once customers are segmented they can be tiered by the costs of serving them well. Some segments will require infrequent contact with the landlord others frequent contact. Some services like repairs will need to be capable of serving different segments in different ways, whilst others, such as personal debt counselling, will only be used for particular well defined segments.

- **Expectation Analysis.**   Focus research on what customers expect now and in the future rather than levels of satisfaction with the past. Whilst all service satisfaction surveys and complaints analysis can help highlight major service problems, qualitative surveys using open ended questions and focus groups will yield more valuable intelligence about expectations. Follow this up with more specific research but concentrate on surveying those customers with recent service experience so that you are measuring service performance not general perception. Survey frequently to keep track of changes in expectations and integrate the findings into other performance measures so that senior management's perception of consumer expectations is kept in line with actual expectations. Experiment with different techniques including relatively sophisticated behavioural management techniques that can unearth what really matters to customers at moments of truth in service delivery.

- **Conditioning.** In researching expectations use the opportunity to influence customers to expect a service that can be delivered within the political, policy and cost constraints under which social landlords work. Also, try to influence them to expect a little less service than can be delivered. The way focus groups are set up and run and the way questionnaires are structured is important, since they provide an opportunity to get across a clear message about the constraints under which the landlord works. Use publicity material such as handbooks, tenant newsletters and service leaflets to influence expectations.

- **Benchmarking.** As part of the research find out what other organisations do. Use focus groups and questionnaires to find out about a tenant or applicants good or bad experience of other organisations. This will need to include experiences of other social landlords where that experience exists, but it can also include experience of service functions provided by non-housing agencies which are similar to services provided by a social landlord.

A successful customer service strategy will succeed if it is rooted in a thorough knowledge of what customers expect and will fail if it is rooted in what managers think customers expect, so social landlords need to become obsessed with listening. Once expectations are clearly established, the next step is to introduce management techniques which enable an organisation to develop quality service specifications and delivery procedures which consistently meet expectations.

CHAPTER 8:
QUALITY MANAGEMENT AND
CUSTOMER SERVICE

Introduction

This chapter will consider:

- The spread of quality management and the range of quality systems and tools that have been developed and applied in the private sector. In this survey the potential and limitations of those systems and tools to support customer service will be reviewed.

- A model, combining these systems and tools which could act as a powerful support to a customer service strategy. This model will be based on the best approaches adopted in the private service sector and will consider in particular the use of the two most widely known quality tools, BS5750 and TQM.

- Approaches to communication with customers. Service organisations deliver their 'product' through communication – written, telephone and face to face – and even the best designed services cannot deliver customer satisfaction if communication is poorly handled.

The Spread of Quality Management

Effective customer service strategies require positive management. Those that excel at customer service organise their business for customer service, try and create a culture which has customer service at the centre of everything they do, and introduce management systems and techniques which directly or indirectly promote quality and customer service. There are as many approaches to the management of customer service as there are companies concerned about it. The common denominator is some kind of quality programme. That is a planned and positive approach to introduce tools and techniques which will focus the organisation on the quality of their products and services. Quality in this context can mean a variety of things – fitness for purpose, conformance to specification, giving the customer what they need, or delighting the customer with products and services that will surprise them. In customer service terms, of course, it is the last definition of quality that is most powerful. Whatever definition is used, the important point is that in organisations with quality programmes, the driving force becomes quality, or at least quality takes its place alongside productivity

Chartered Institute of Housing

and return on investment as the guiding principles of effective management.

It is the manufacturing sector that has taken the lead in developing and introducing quality management as the means to customer satisfaction. In particular the Japanese have pioneered most of the approaches now being adopted in the west. The service sector has been much slower to adopt such techniques but they are beginning to catch up. Leading service companies like British Airways or American Express have been applying all embracing quality programmes for more than a decade. Such programmes are designed to ensure services are of the highest quality as the essential pre-requisite for satisfying customers. In these companies customer service is what drives everybody from top to bottom, and their managers are always looking to bias action towards quality. Colin Marshall, in the early days at British Airways, when he was trying to make it the service leader, used to ignore reports or requests that were not about customer service. His staff soon learned that if they wanted to get something past him they would have to build a customer service argument into the submission. (Smith, 1989 p 70)

Where the likes of British Airways led, many other service organisations are now following. In the United Kingdom, the health sector, service giants like British Telecom, the banks and building societies, larger retail companies and distribution companies are all embarking on some kind of customer centred quality programme. These companies know that it is no good listening to the customer and raising expectations as to what can be delivered if the company does not develop the right customer centred culture and introduce systems and tools which enable staff to deliver the quality services promised. British Rail is pursuing a strategy of trying to refocus this huge organisation to customer service. It is proving an uphill struggle since it has a deep seated reputation for poor service quality, has suffered for years from under investment and has an ingrained culture and systems that can only be changed slowly. New promotions, advertising slogans and declared performance targets are successfully raising expectations but follow up changes within British Rail are much slower in delivering to those expectations. Dr Steve Smith, a leading quality consultant, has commented with sympathy on British Rail's dilemma.

> "I heard that British Rail's Intercity Service was employing attractive young women to mingle with irate passengers on over crowded trains in an attempt to pacify them. A wonderful example of a doomed 'fix it' approach. We cannot solve it at source, so add on more and more to try and suppress the symptoms, like a field service force constantly repairing vacuum cleaners that were poorly designed." (Smith 1989 p 70)

Social housing has been slower than most of the service sector in embracing quality programmes. They are closer to British Rail than they are to British Airways. The reasons for this are not dissimilar to those which have constrained the adoption of sophisticated market research techniques. Lack of choice for tenants creates limited incentive to change from old ways of doing things. The general hostility of the housing manager to the use of the product and profit centred approaches of the private sector in a unique people centred social service. But as with market research, social housing organisations could learn a lot from the private sector in the value and use of quality programmes as useful management techniques to support customer service strategies.

Quality Management Tools and Customer Service

Gap Analysis

Gap analysis provides as useful a framework in relation to the application of quality management tools as it does in respect of market research. As outlined in the last chapter the biggest underlying cause of customer dissatisfaction is the communication gaps where managers have incorrect views of customer needs and expectations (Gap 1), and the wrong external signals are communicated such as promises of service performance which cannot be met (Gap 4). These gaps are closed through effective market research. Also in the suppliers domain are two other gaps. One is where management gives misleading signals to staff about the standards required and the tasks to be carried out (Gap 2). This is the leadership gap in which managers, having become aware of customer expectations, do not create the right culture or strategy to deliver to those expectations. The other is when actual service delivery processes do not enable the agreed standards and specifications for services to be met. (Gap 3)

Over the last 60 years and particularly the last 20 years, manufacturing industry has developed a wide variety of quality management tools and techniques. They have become widespread because they are recognised as powerful weapons to gain competitive advantage by "getting things right first time every time", and in so doing delight the customers and reduce production costs. More recently the private service sector has adopted these same tools for the same reasons. It is clear that, if appropriately used, they can significantly contribute to an effective customer service strategy by closing some of the key service gaps in the suppliers domain.

The Tools and Techniques

Different tools and techniques, whether by design or not, are better suited to closing one gap rather than another. Some of the tools and techniques have proved more suitable to the particular problems of service organisations than others. Some tools used in combination will have more of an impact on customer service than if used in isolation. Occasionally these tools and techniques have evolved from older well tried approaches to management, training or production control with quality of service as the driver rather than an objective such as return on investment. They may even be given new, exotic labels to help promote them as the heroic solution for a company's quality problems. However, notwithstanding such promotional tricks, even old management tools can take on a new value if recast, mixed with other new ingredients and targeted in new ways.

The tools and techniques that have a particular role in contributing to a customer service strategy fall into three main categories. Those that can be used to improve process control so that any product or service that is delivered is well designed, fit for purpose, defect free and is reliable whoever is responsible for its manufacture or, in the case of services, its delivery. Those that help in the way the 'moments of truth' are handled when customers and staff interact. Those that help to create a whole new culture and set of attitudes which put the customer first and make delighting the customer the primary objective of the organisation. There are a long list of tools and techniques which are now deployed. The main ones to be considered here are

CATEGORY	QUALITY MANAGEMENT TECHNIQUE
Process Control:	Quality Control (QC)
	Quality Assurance (QA)
	Business Process Re-engineering (BPR)
	Statistical Process Control (SPC)
	Service Design Tools
	Quality Circles
	Total Quality Management (TQM)
Moments of Truth:	Customer Care
	Total Quality Management
Culture Change:	Total Quality Management

Some of the tools and techniques cross the boundaries of these three categories and those which address culture, notably Total Quality Management, seek to tackle everything from leadership, through process control to customer interaction.

Quality Control

Quality Control is simply the function of checking for errors during and after the process of manufacture. In social housing it is particularly applicable as part of the system to build a new home and is usually undertaken by a clerk of works. In the repairs service it is one of the roles of a maintenance supervisor. Quality Control puts a heavy reliance on inspectors and whilst it helps to identify errors during or after a product, like a house, or a service, like repairs, is produced, it does not prevent them arising in the first place. It puts poor quality right after the event and whilst a customer will want a faulty product or service corrected when things go wrong, a more effective tool is that which ensures reliability of a product or service before it is delivered.

Quality Assurance: BS5750

From Quality Control there has developed Quality Assurance. This is a process to ensure that all attempts are made to reduce non-conformance to a service or product specification. It's focus is on prevention and involves a combination of carefully specified procedures, and measurement systems to pick up non-conformance. The most noted quality assurance system is BS5750, also known as ISO 9000. This standard is a form of accreditation that an organisation's management systems can be relied upon to deliver the same product or service whoever does it. In the context of customer service and gap analysis, a quality assurance tool such as BS5750 can help tackle the gap between the specification of service quality and actual service delivery, but it does not tackle the other gaps. It is a fairly mechanistic tool which can only help in the processes leading up to service delivery, not the moment of truth of service delivery. It also tends to be narrowly focused on improving existing functional procedures of a particular department. If those procedures are based on a service specification which does not meet customer expectations then a Quality Assurance tool like BS5750 will not help the fundamental problem of an inappropriate specification. BS5750 is becoming a popular entry point into quality programmes and is discussed in more detail later in this chapter.

Business Process Re-Engineering (BPR)

This is one of the newer members of the family of quality management tools. It is a distant cousin of Quality Assurance and has much greater potential in helping to deliver effective customer service. Alternatively known as Business Process Management or Business Process Re-design, it is an approach to procedure design which breaks out of the narrow functional approach common in most organisations to an approach which focuses on key processes which run across many functions. Such processes are usually tackled in small bits, with a particular function dealing with that part of the process which falls within their domain. The problem is that key parts of the process are not managed directly because they fall between a number of functions, all of which have higher priorities.

Nobody takes responsibility for the whole process leading to the delivery of a service or product to the customer. To take a couple of examples from social housing. The letting of a property involves a process which starts with the termination of a tenancy, continues through an inspection and maintenance function to becoming available for re-let to letting. The lettings section or staff responsible for allocation can make their processes effective, but may not be able to control the processes up to that point. Their ability to serve the customer with a satisfactory home which is made available quickly, depends on other functions. Another example is the rent control process, akin to the billing process in many companies. From a tenants perspective they want the right rent, charged at the right time, amended through strict rules with easy ways to pay, clear information about the state of their account with the right housing benefit and other help with payment if necessary. The process can involve several functions – housing management, computer services, finance, housing benefit and welfare advice. There is an enormous opportunity to create cumbersome, ill fitting procedures which have a high error rate, complex paper flows and are generally designed with little consideration for the customer. Business Process Re-engineering involves the meticulous mapping of the total process and then, and this is the key feature, the rigorous challenging of the process. Is this step adding value or waste? Can we go directly from here to there and cut out these activities? Is there a better way?

As described in Chapter 7, American Express was used in relation to their research into customer expectation on issuing new cards and identified that the swift replacement of cards was a key expectation. They applied this technique to the problem and by systematically improving and managing the process of new card issue they reduced the time from 20 days to 5 days making them a saving of 70 million and substantially improving customer satisfaction. The horror stories of the last few years on practices and procedures for managing housing benefit and the hardship that was created for many people in the process might have been avoided if a tool such as Business Process Re-engineering had been deployed. The more advanced quality companies now manage their businesses more by processes than functions. At IBM they assign process ownership at vice-president level, to establish responsibility for the key processes as well as functional responsibilities. BPR is a process control system like BS5750 and cannot tackle the interaction with the customer, but it has enormous potential to speed up and improve key processes making that moment of interaction easier to handle. Taken to its logical conclusion it can suggest radical approaches to organisation structures replacing function based structures with process based ones. In particular it can result in an approach which breaks down central service functions and leads to the distribution of staff amongst service delivery departments. In social housing agencies it could challenge the time honoured approach to housing management based on individual housing officers trying to manage many functions on behalf of a group of tenants and suggest an approach which is process based.

Statistical Process Control

This is another technique which is designed to help in process control so that systems and procedures deliver consistent products and services, and so again its value to a customer service strategy is in closing the gap between service quality specifications and service delivery. Statistical Process Control has a long history going back to the pioneer work of two statisticians in the 1920s, Walter Shewhat and W. Edwards Deming. The basic principle of this tool is to apply statistical techniques to see if a process is in or out of statistical control, in other words whether something is running smoothly. If there are large deviations because of unexplained special causes, these have to be identified and eliminated so that the variation that remains can be attributed to the process itself. The importance of SPC in customer service strategies is not simply the statistical monitoring of a process, but its use to drive improvements by reducing variation and in this way improving quality. Once special causes of statistical variation have been eliminated, only common causes remain and improvement can be brought about by management action. This is because the variation that remains is due to the way that the processes and systems have been designed and built. One of the leading quality gurus, Joseph Juran, has estimated that no more than 15% of the problems, or variation in an organisation are due to special causes, leaving management with the responsibility for at least 85% of potential improvement through changes on the system within which their staff have to work. This technique has been widely used in manufacturing industry but it can be used in services. In the context of housing, a service such as repairs can be subjected to this kind of discipline. A medium sized landlord with 2,000 to 3,000 units would have 10,000 to 15,000 repairs a year. These repairs need to be completed within a particular period which would vary depending on whether the repair is an emergency, urgent or normal. The organisation would have in place a procedure to handle each type of repair to achieve that standard. SPC could be used to monitor the statistical variation in response times. If unusual causes such as a run of burst pipes in a cold spell, or a reduction in staff are eliminated, and the control statistics still show a wide variation in response times then the process is out of control and needs improvement. Only if the variation is reduced and the process brought back under control can the service be deemed reliable and hope to meet one of the major customer requirements of any service. SPC has a strong track record of working very well, even in service areas. But to be successful it requires total commitment and someone who can explain the use of statistics simply.

Service Design Tools

One of the sophisticated quality tools pioneered by Japanese manufacturers and adopted by western manufacturers for designing products is known as Quality Function Deployment. It is used by motor manufacturers to ensure that the 'voice of the customer' is met by design requirements and in the manufacturing and assembly process. Co-incidentally, a key tool in this process is a relationship chart commonly known as 'the house of quality'. This relationship chart is designed to translate what the customer wants into how it is to be achieved in design. The chart is a matrix with customer requirements set at right angles to design and performance proposals. The customer requirements are established by using a variety of customer-orientated techniques to establish expectations and priorities. A relationship is then plotted where a design and performance element intersects a customer requirement. This relationship is usually determined on a simple grading of small, medium or strong. If a known customer requirement does not have a relationship with any design or performance element then the design is incomplete, and if a design or performance element does not have a relationship with any customer requirement then the design feature is uncalled for. The chart also includes the ability to correlate different design requirements in the 'roof' of the house of quality and it also has the facility to incorporate customer and technical ratings of a competitors product. This technique has proved an extremely powerful one in balancing the potentially conflicting relationships of new product design, customer expectations, product performance, costs and service issues. It is clearly highly sophisticated and would be daunting, if not difficult, to deploy in a social housing organisation. There is clearly some scope for experimenting with 'the house of quality' to see if it could be applied to the process of establishing a brief and performance specification for a house or flat. An effective customer service strategy ought to start with the possibility of delighting the customer with the home for which they pay rent.

Its application to the design of services and the processes behind the delivery of services is less obvious, but the principles behind it could be effectively used in services. When a service is designed the process is usually haphazard. It is often a quick leap from

> "… a very ill-formed and ill critiqued idea of a service immediately into assembling and launching the service into the market place". (Gummesson 1990, p 97)

There are now attempts to translate this kind of controlled design technique to services. One such technique is known as service blue printing which is a systematic way of describing a service in the form of a flow chart 'blue print' which considers the inter dependence in a service activity of people, products, paper flows, cost and contribution to revenue and those parts of the service which are most sensitive to errors. Another technique is called SOS, which stands for Strategy and Organisation for Service. It is a quality tree which follows a specific design process as follows:

* a group of people with knowledge of a particular service discuss its parts and the factors influencing the quality of the service.

* a computer programme builds a tree structure where the conclusions of

the group are gradually ordered and revised.

* each component of this tree structure is then assessed with respect to its affect on quality and the ability of the organisation to perform. This can also be done in comparison with competing companies.

* a print out is produced showing the quality tree and the significance of the quality influencing factors.

The use of tools of this kind is beginning to find a wider interest in the service sector. In 1993 a conference was held in London on the use of Quality Function Deployment and other service design tools for companies in retail and financial services and it included the experience of organisations like Abbey National and Lloyds Bank. In applying these service design tools Evert Gummesson, Professor of Service Management at the Service Research Centre at Karlstad in Sweden, highlights key elements

* use systematic procedures for service design to a larger extent than is normal today.

* get inspiration from the systematic design approaches used in manufacturing industries, but do not force them where inappropriate, rather allow services to thrive on their own design conditions.

* service design must allow for the fact that two groups interact in service – the employees of the provider and the customers. In some cases a highly standardised interaction is preferable (e.g. rent payment) sometimes each situation is highly unique and dependent on human contact.

* the design must give room for the employees to act on the spur of the moment so that they can use their personalities to solve problems in the interest of the customer and the employee. (Gummesson, 1990)

Quality Circles

A concept like Quality Function Deployment is almost certainly going to bring about a glazed expression on the average housing director and the cynical response 'not another fancy consultants tool'. In contrast the Quality Circle is something which has a more familiar ring. It was one of the first of the Japanese management tools to have been adopted by western companies. It is now familiar in western manufacturing and services and there are a variety of approaches. The Japanese way is for there to be groups of people, often structured on normal work groups, who meet on a voluntary basis, together with their direct supervisor to discuss 'improvements'. Another approach is to go for non voluntary circles which can cut across functions because most quality improvement opportunities lie outside the natural work group. One of the leading quality gurus, Philip Crosby, promotes the concept of Error Cause Removal Teams or Corrective Action Teams formed as needed with members drawn from various functions to tackle a specific problem and disband when the problem is solved. Quality circles also mesh with a concept like Business Process Re-engineering since this requires multi-functional teams to map business processes (as opposed to department processes) and re-design and improve them.

A quality circle – whether based on a normal work group or involving people from different functions – will need training in problem solving tools such as Brainstorming, Ishikawa or Fishbone analysis and Pereto Analysis. Their strength is that they are a 'bottom up' strategy for improving processes involving the staff who have to work within the system and so often know the faults better than supervisors and managers. However, a great number of initiatives have failed.

Tom Peters, whilst emphasising the value of quality circles as a tool for improvements that will delight customers, also highlights the problems that lead to failure. These include, amongst others, misunderstanding of the concept by management creating false expectations, sabotage by middle managers who see their role challenged by these teams, poor training for participants and failure to implement proposals. In a typically graphic example he refers to his experience of the views of workers in

> "the so called humanized/humanistic Silicon Valley. I'm here to tell you that in six out of seven companies that I visit in that valley, Mecca of twenty-first-century management, the average worker wouldn't attend his or her next quality circle meeting if it was the last day on earth. They see it for exactly what it is : another way for management to jerk labour's chain."
> (Peters et al 1986, p 101)

Customer Care

With Customer Care we shift from techniques that focus on the design of services and improving processes behind services to techniques designed to help at 'moments of truth' in the customer supplier relationship. Process control and improvement can be of little value if, during the 15 second interaction between a customer and a staff member when the customer can make up their mind about a company, the staff member is discourteous, vague, has no empathy with the customer, leaves them feeling they are the enemy, or displays lack of knowledge about their problems or the service they are looking for. Effective customer care programmes are not about public relations – telling the customer how great they are by using advertising. Philip Atkinson in his book 'Creating Culture Change' refers to a company in financial services that spent a great deal on a TV campaign focusing upon their speedy response to the customer. 8,000 disgruntled viewers wrote to complain that their experiences did not match this.

"The company recognised that it had a major problem and that it had to improve the service through action not advertising". (Atkinson, 1990 p 15)

Effective customer care programmes also reject the concept of the customer service department. Customer service departments are

"... the limbo to which employees assign those problems that they refuse to solve themselves" and they can often "... degrade service by acting as shields to protect companies from customers' problems". (Davidow et al 1989 pp 104-5)

Effective customer care is based on educating everybody about customer service and specifically changing the attitudes of 'boundary personnel', the people who come into contact with the customer. Most good customer care programmes focus on the non-quantifiable nature of service. This includes tangibles – the office reception and the appearance of staff; reliability – the expectation customers have of dependable, accurate and consistent service; responsiveness – the readiness and willingness to serve customers promptly and efficiently, assurance – the courtesy and competence of personnel that instils confidence in customers; and empathy – individual attention and caring for the customers' personal needs. Customer care programmes are, first and foremost, about effective communication. The telephone conversation, the face to face conversation in the home or in the office and written communication – leaflets, handbooks and letters – are the fundamental activities by which 'boundary personnel' actually deliver their well designed, quality assured services. Of course just as efforts to improve processes can founder on a poorly handled moment of truth; so a well handled moment of truth is of little value if the processes behind services cannot be relied upon. The overall quality provided to the customer is still poor except that a facade has been built to temporarily shield the customer. Customer care programmes, like BS5750, are a common entry point into quality management for many service organisations, including social landlords.

Total Quality Management

Total Quality Management is something of a portmanteau phrase which is much abused. It is used to cover a variety of different approaches to quality. The roots of conventional TQM are in Quality Control and Quality Assurance. It has also absorbed the 'excellence' movement driven hard by Tom Peters. In the last few years it has come to mean a set of attitudes about customer service and excellence with, behind it, a raft of managerial systems all designed to promote and support quality in the design, production and service of products and services. In this way a TQM programme is an umbrella for all or just some of the systems and tools described above.

Dr John Nichols has written extensively on the evolution of TQM and the difficulties of defining what it is. He has identified four incarnations. Initially he notes that TQM focused on the concept of quality as conformance to specification. It was a combination of Quality Control, Quality Assurance and measurement techniques like SPC applied systematically to ensure an organisations' management and production systems delivered products and services to a consistent standard. In its second incarnation the focus shifted to quality as fitness for purpose in which the product or service does what it is supposed to do. This required the involvement of the whole organisation in error free work through positive leadership to ensure a product or service was delivered right first time every time and on time. The third incarnation was quality as what the customer wants. This version focused on the importance of the customer as the only one who can effectively define needs. It introduced the concept of the internal customer. In the first incarnation the focus was on the product made or service provided, and it tended to ignore those not directly involved in the production or delivery process. The concept of the clerical administrative and support people as internal customers in a quality delivery process helped to overcome this remoteness. In the same way, external suppliers were also brought into the process. Finally, the fourth and most recent incarnation is quality as adding value to the customer and delighting them. The focus here is on engaging everyone in competitive delivery of value to the customer through transforming leadership, the empowerment of staff, value adding process streams, and competitive benchmarking. (Nichols, 1992)

The distinguishing features of TQM are that it does and must embrace everybody in the organisation. It requires continuous improvement – quality as a never ending journey. It is not cost cutting but quality will inevitably be cheaper. Most important it puts the customer at the centre of everything that is done and it requires a whole new culture. In the words of Keith Milum, TQM manager for Harris Distribution, a major transport group,

> "Total Quality Management is undoubtedly more difficult to get to grips with as it is more a question of attitude than process. Total Quality Management emphasises the nature of customers; how important meeting their requirement is; the importance of commitment to getting it right first time; calculation of error costs, and teams as a means of reaching solutions to problems". (Milum 1990 p 5–7)

It is thus right at the centre of useful techniques that can help in a customer service strategy.

Some Problems in Applying Quality Management Techniques

Nearly all of these tools have emerged from the manufacturing sector, and many of them derive from Japanese management methods. They all have their various champions. Some of the tools are over promoted by management consultants as speedy and heroic solutions to gain increased market share through a revolution in quality. The better informed are more patient evangelists of their careful application as part of a change in management culture which requires patience, persistence and leadership. For every champion there is also a critic. The successes of Ford, Rank Xerox and Rover in the manufacturing sector, and American Express and British Airways in the service sector, are necessarily balanced by many other companies who have not found the quality path paved with gold. In April 1992 two surveys, one by Arthur D Little in the USA and one by A T Kearney in 'The TQM Magazine' in the United Kingdom, showed that in a significant number of cases total quality programmes implemented by companies in recent years had failed to produce the level of tangible results and the competitive advantage that they had hoped for. In the context of customer service strategies and specifically in relation to the service sector, the criticisms of the value of these tools revolves around three issues:

*   Excessively system based and tool bound.
*   Satisfaction with the quick fix.
*   Inappropriate to the service sector.

Excessively System-based and tool bound

The tools and systems described above are merely a means to an end, but it is very easy for them to become an end in themselves. As one commentator has put it

> "when measurement charts are being used as an alternative to wallpaper, it is a reasonable bet that nothing much will change…"
> (Macdonald 1992 p 239)

Even where managers are not merely attracted by the charts and control manuals, they do not always see the importance of the way such systems have to mesh with other human and leadership factors. Another commentator warns of the problem of

> "… only lip service being given to the importance of people and the harnessing of their full potential. The holy trio of Maslow, Heinzberg and MacGregor is invoked before rapidly getting down to the business of installing the systems. Even service organisations are prone to this lingering systems bias." (Nichols 1990 p 86)

Systems bias can also result in a tendency to put energy into only one or perhaps two of the tools and in so doing invest them with a potential power to deliver quality that they do not have. In the United Kingdom the BS5750 quality assurance system has been severely abused and misused by companies and consultants as the easiest and quickest route to quality management. Customers are now frequently promised a quality product or service because it is BS5750 approved. Many large companies have become almost tyrannical in their insistence that their suppliers also obtain BS5750 for their management systems.

There is a danger that by overpromoting, misusing and abusing some of these tools the noted adage – a bad workman always blames his tools and in blaming them rejects them as useless – will come true. These various tools need to be applied appropriately, selectively and collectively. Any one of them can be an entry point into quality management and improved customer service, but they need to be seen as part of a customer value stream which starts with customer research to establish expectations, moves through the careful design and specification of products and services, to get them right and consistent, to the actual interaction with the customer at the point of sale and service. The whole thing has to be positively lead by a management committed to quality. No one tool can do all of this.

Satisfaction with the 'Quick Fix'

One of the reasons that companies concentrate on one or two of the tools is that they are looking for a quick fix. The approach to quality, particularly in the west, goes something like this: the executives of a company want to do something about quality because they have heard that it will save them money and increase their market share. They pick on a tool or a programme, usually one neatly packaged by a consultant, and hope that in two or three years by devoting their attention to this problem, they will get quality right, satisfy their customers and save money.

Paul Davies, Director of TQM International Ltd, has commented wryly on this approach.

> "The expectation of unrealistic short term benefits lies behind the untimely demise of a number of TQM processes. To say that nobody should expect to perform in two years what it has taken others decades to achieve may seem to be a statement of the obvious, but it is a message that has still yet to be widely understood. I still get phone calls from people who say they would like to 'get their company through TQM' and ask when we can do it for them! ... asking at the start, 'How long is all this going to take?' Can too often be an early sign that significant achievement could be elusive."
> (Davies 1992 p 201)

Quality circles, BS5750 and Customer Care are the classic quick fix short cuts companies have tried in order to "get their company through" it. Quality circles were seen as the 'magic elixir' which transformed Japan. They appealed to western managers because they were relatively cheap to organise and they placed the responsibility for quality where managers thought it belonged, with the worker. As Tom Peters noted, the workers were having none of this and the quality circle movement quickly foundered. Customer care programmes have been the quick fix solution for service organisations. Polite receptionists, a courteous telephone manner and apologising when a mistake is made are all elements in quality service, but if they merely serve to paper over the cracks of a back office that is out of control then they are of little long term value. Saying sorry is fine as long as you do not keep having to do it. As commented earlier, BS5750 is now in danger of becoming a casualty of the quick fix mentality.

Inappropriate to the service sector

The service sector has been much slower to give attention to the issue of quality in the design and delivery of their services. Since this sector has been relatively backward, they have, inevitably, tried to draw on the experience of manufacturing. The management consultants, keen to expand their client base, have also been quick to push quality tools into service companies arguing that the principles apply to services as well as to products. The counter to this is that whilst these quality tools and systems are beneficial, if used in the right way, they do not handle the special characteristics of service. Because of their manufacturing background, the argument goes, quality tools are defined in product terms and are used to produce pre-set standards. Quality management is what you do before the customer gets involved. It is accepted that these tools can help in some aspects of service design. In particular they can be applied to the deliverables of service quality. In housing management this would include such things as the accuracy of details on rent accounts, the time taken to do a repair, the number of repeat repairs, the speed of processing an application for a home or for housing benefit and the level of complaints. But, ultimately, services are intangible, production and delivery is simultaneous and you have little opportunity to inspect before you deliver. These criticisms, however, have resulted in further developments of quality management systems to make them more suitable to the service sector. Building on the successful experiences of major service organisations such as British Airways the traditional process driven quality management systems have been adapted and expanded to ensure that the approach adopted focuses on the customer and the peculiarities of service. An edition of the 'TQM Magazine' in February 1989 was called 'The service sector responds to the quality challenge' and was wholly given over to guidance and case studies on the way various quality tools might be used in service organisations.

Whilst recognising the limitations of traditional manufacturing based quality management, the message was that service company managers should build on what has been done in the manufacturing sector rather than just blindly following in its footsteps. There is certainly enough experience in the service sector for an effective approach, or model, to be described which would enable a service sector like social housing to exploit many of these quality management tools and in so doing have a better chance of defining and delivering an effective customer service strategy.

Applying Quality Management — A Model for Social Housing

TQM vs BS5750

As quality programmes proliferate, there has been a tendency for two camps to emerge in both the manufacturing and private service sectors based on two distinct implementation strategies. The two approaches are one which focuses on overall culture change and one which is a more fragmented project by project approach. One manifestation of this is the Total Quality Management approach versus BS5750. The first of these requires a long term commitment with the possibility of a lot of early pain without much gain. The second can produce quicker results with a part of an organisations' procedures becoming quality assured fairly quickly and then the incremental extension of this to other procedures. In terms of a model approach which can address customer service overall, this dichotomy is artificial. Service organisations that have been successful in their application of quality management tools apply both techniques. British Telecom, for example, are aiming to bring about a culture change through a Total Quality Management programme, but they also have been tackling problems on a project by project basis. The obvious example of this being the way they have improved the public telephone service. However, whilst emphasising the value of both techniques a model approach needs to be based on Total Quality Management. BS5750 primarily has value as a building block within a Total Quality Management programme.

In social housing the debate on the best approach is just beginning but there is evidence that this dichotomy is already beginning to emerge. Both the National Federation of Housing Associations and the Institute of Housing have taken up the issue of quality management tools and through their journals, publications and conferences have encouraged debate on different approaches to quality. The NFHA have launched a series of publications on the theme of quality and customer service. One of them deals with complaints, but significantly the first one in the series is a guide to BS5750. The Institute of Housing whilst seeing the value of BS5750, has been more cautious about backing any particular approach. Their effort has gone into trying to establish a set of management standards for housing management. However, it may be significant that they have published a guide to Total Quality Management in their professional practice series. The issue of quality has also been the subject of a publication by the Housing Management Advisory Panel for Wales. Again BS5750 features in this document although it does not promote it as the only or even primary route to quality.

BS5750 and Customer Service

It is significant that BS5750 accreditation appears so prominently in these publications, for this reflects the views and approaches of the members of these organisations. There are a handful of social landlords who have decided to adopt or investigate the more holistic TQM approach. CCHA Housing based in the Midlands adopted a TQM programme in 1989. John Huckett of Cranfield Institute of Technology has also been involved with a handful of other housing agencies considering TQM including Enfield Council, Liverpool Housing Trust and the Welsh Federation of Housing Associations. However, there is a much larger group of housing associations and local authorities who have decided to go down the BS5750 route. In the Spring of 1992 the management consultants, Cooper Bassett carried out a survey on the attitude of local housing authorities to BS5750. They interviewed a sample of 28 local authorities, 40% were planning to apply for BS5750. The reasons for applying included the desire for a competitive advantage in the face of compulsory competitive tendering, good public relations and the desire to guarantee the level of service quality to customers. Since this survey there has been a regular flow of news items in the housing press featuring social landlords who have achieved the BS5750 standard. These include Braintree, Hertsmere and Alyn and Deeside Councils and the Midlands housing association, 'Focus'. Cooper Bassett's own newsletters also report that a number of others are actively seeking or considering the kitemark including South East Lancashire Housing Association, Sanctuary Housing Association and Network Housing Association.

Given the prominence of BS5750 amongst those landlords pioneering quality programmes it is worth looking at this tool in more detail, and its place in a model approach to quality management and customer service.

BS5750 is a nationally accepted standard for quality assurance. It is a management standard. Whereas other standards set a specification (such as BS7070 for lead free petrol), BS5750 addresses the processes needed to ensure that a level of service or a product consistently meets a prescribed standard. However it does not set the standard and this is an important point to keep in mind. It is a quality assurance tool designed to prevent errors occurring in the delivery of services or products by assuring the management processes that control a deliverable output such as a repairs service. It has the designation BS5750 because the procedures meet a British Standard. In Europe the accreditation reference is EN 29000 and internationally it is ISO9000. Registration is achieved and maintained using an independent third party assessor who monitors the recipient of the standard to ensure they are applying the quality assured procedures used to produce a service or product. BS5750 was created by the Ministry of Defence where precise specifications for products have been set for a long time. The Ministry of Defence found that, despite the very tight levels of specification and post production inspection, unacceptably high levels of failure were still being experienced. By addressing the issue of process they hoped that expensive post production inspection could be reduced.

BS5750, like most quality assurance systems, addresses processes. It does not set the specification for quality of output. However, to ensure that levels of quality prescribed are consistently met, BS5750 requires a number of management procedures to be addressed and documented to demonstrate control. The standard has several parts. Part 0.1 is a guide to the selection and use of the appropriate part of the BS5750 series. Part 0.2 is a guide to overall quality management and the quality system – elements within the BS5750 series. Part 1 relates to quality specifications for design, production, installation and servicing when the requirements of products or services are specified. Part 2 sets out the requirements where a firm is manufacturing goods or offering a service to a published specification. Part 3 specifies the quality system to be used in any test and inspection procedures. A service sector such as social housing would primarily be concerned with part 1. Part 2 may be applicable if a housing association or local authority has an architectural department or perhaps in the context of services provided to a voluntary agency managing a special project on behalf of a housing association or local authority.

The standard itself requires that written control procedures are in place in respect of twenty elements including, amongst others, management responsibility, document control, purchasing, process control, inspection, control of services which do not conform to the normal standard, quality records, internal quality audits, training and statistical techniques. Once a service has gone through the BS5750 disciplines, the organisation will have four levels of documentation. A statement of aim in the form of a quality policy; a general statement of what will be done to achieve the aim in the form of a quality manual; a set of detailed statements of how a process should be performed in the form of a set of procedures and these procedures broken down further into work instructions.

An implementation strategy for a BS5750 system would typically follow five key stages:

The first stage is an evaluation exercise in which an assessment is made as to what exists compared to what is required by the standard. At this stage the standard has to be understood, existing procedures established and matched against the standards' requirements, an implementation project team set up, commitment of the senior staff obtained, and a clear set of quality policies and objectives agreed and communicated.

The second stage is to prepare a set of agreed procedures which cover all the processes. A standard format for these procedures needs to be agreed which must be able to be controlled and structured for ease of use. Procedures should be carefully tested for relevance and accuracy by those who have to operate them. Procedures will also need a controlling authority within the organisation who sign off all procedures.

The third stage is implementation. Everybody using the procedures needs to be trained and a control system for amending and updating procedures and keeping staff trained in the procedures put in place.

The fourth stage is auditing. The standard requires that formal audit procedures are included to monitor the application of the procedures and that any problems encountered are addressed so that small incremental improvements take place continuously within the business processes. In essence this systems auditing performs the same role as financial audit of accounts. It checks both the adequacy of the system and the accuracy of records kept from that system. It also controls corrections of and changes to procedures as new ways of doing things are introduced.

The final stage is external assessment and accreditation. An external accreditation agency will independently check that the procedures meet the BS5750 standard and then register the service as BS5750 approved. They will also make periodic surveillance visits to ensure the procedures remain appropriate and properly applied.

BS5750 is undoubtedly a rigorous quality assurance system. It has the attractions of a packaged solution to establishing quality assured procedures which can be installed, with or without outside help, in a relatively short time. In a typical housing environment a full programme could be implemented in between 12 and 18 months. It also has the attraction that it can be applied incrementally. A BS5750 project can be implemented on one service such as repairs, and then in a series of steps applied to other deliverable services until the whole housing management function is covered. It can also be used to discipline internal functions such as computer systems or financial services. Finally, the external accreditation process imposes a useful external discipline as well as having a high public relations value. Its use in public relations has to be handled carefully. Many companies have over promoted their acquisition of BS5750 and implied that this means they are a recognised quality company when in fact they might only have had BS5750 on one part of their organisation. If a social landlord has achieved accreditation on, say, its application service, all this proves is that they have quality assured procedures for handling applicants it does not mean they have a quality housing management service.

As a quality assurance system it also has the potential for introducing other quality management principles in its wake. If introduced in the context of actually trying to raise quality standards and improve customer service rather than just to get a good public relations tool, then aspects of the requirement and the way it is introduced can be beneficial. For example, the requirement to be specific about quality policy and the objectives of a set of procedures creates the opportunity to set high standards and, if customer expectations are well understood, standards that will delight the customer. An effective implementation strategy will help in building teamwork and ensuring staff on the front line can adequately contribute to the development of effective processes. Also the requirement to measure will encourage a mentality of continual improvement of processes.

But, in the context of a customer service strategy care is needed not to over endow it with a power it does not possess. The heart of BS5750 is the control and documentation of any process leading to a service or the manufacture of a product. It will tackle gap 3 in gap analysis – the gap between service quality specification and service delivery – but it is not an effective tool to tackle the other gaps. Moreover, gap 3 is the least significant one in an overall effective customer service strategy. As one commentator has said albeit with mild overstatement

> "The BS5750 approach wholly ignores client perceptions of quality and fails to adequately address client servicing. It focuses on technical quality and administrative systems … not the improvement of client quality" (Moore 1992 p 68)

Stephen Halliday of 'The Observer' makes the same point more colourfully.

> "A few days ago, I received an advertising mailshot from a car windscreen replacement service. I had not heard of the company before but, on the bottom of the mailshot the reassuring words, 'The BS5750 Quality Assured Service' were prominently printed. Had I not known better, I would have taken this as a British Standards Seal of Approval, indicating a high standard of product and service. But it could mean the standards set will guarantee a poor product, a poor service and the need for another windscreen a week later". (Halliday 1993)

This comment highlights the particular problem that if the initial specification does not meet customer expectations then a quality assurance system like BS5750 could actually re-enforce poor quality and service characteristics customers do not want. One company owner vigorously made this point to Clive Woodcock of 'The Guardian'.

> "Application of the standard does not assure quality, only consistency. If the design or manufacturing process is bad and results in an article of poor quality, BS5750 will help to ensure that further articles are made to a consistently poor standard". (Woodcock 1992)

The accreditation process is not actually a necessary part of the quality assurance process. The BS5750 disciplines can be introduced without actually seeking accreditation. Indeed, although accreditation introduces a useful external discipline it can be tyrannical. One of the major themes of press criticism of the standard is that large companies are beginning to impose on their suppliers the requirement that they have the standard. No BS5750, no contract. This has led to exasperation amongst many small businesses. A survey carried out by the Small Business Research Trust in 1992 asked firms if their business was affected by the development of formal quality procedures such as BS5750. An unprecedented 28% replied and 95% of the comments were unfavourable. The principal concern was that BS5750 would raise costs without improving product quality and that many suppliers would be forced out of business because they could not afford certification. (Woodcock 1992)

Local authorities and housing associations keen to adopt the standard, need to be very wary of imposing it on suppliers such as small repairs contractors who can deliver quality services without the burden of BS5750. One of the comments from the survey of small businesses referred to above was that BS5750 was "more bureaucratic nonsense" and "A paperwork standard and not a quality standard". The champions of BS5750 in the public sector generally and social housing in particular need to heed this criticism that it is potentially just another bureaucracy. One of the attractions of BS5750 to them is its bureaucratic characteristics and they are comfortable with it because it re-enforces these familiar and comfortable characteristics. Public services, including local authorities and housing associations, are in a period of rapid and turbulent change. A high degree of flexibility is required to the pull and push of government and customers expecting a better service. In such circumstances organisations have to be customer driven not bureaucracy driven. If all you do with BS5750 is quality assure existing practices then it could result in the entrenchment of a bureaucracy which is inappropriate. This will not benefit a progressive customer service strategy but drive it further away.

BS5750 Case Studies

Notwithstanding these notes of caution, there are good examples of where BS5750 has been used successfully as a positive way of improving customer service. In social housing two of the best examples are concerned with its application to the repairs service. The repairs service is arguably the most important core service of any landlord. By its very nature it requires strict process control since it is a volume activity constrained by strict standards of performance. BS5750 scores in such circumstances. Alyn and Deeside District Council launched a BS5750 project in 1991 in their client side housing repairs service. The reasons for seeking accreditation included the desire to ensure standards in a key part of the housing service which was not under the direct control of the housing department and a desire to strengthen the training culture of the organisation. In selecting this route to quality, Alyn and Deeside were forced to confront the issue of standards and the customer and this has meant understanding what customers expect. An offshoot of this quality assurance initiative has been the development of a customer care policy.

In the Midlands, Focus Housing Association were awarded BS5750 for their repairs service in the summer of 1993. According to Wayne Hughes, Maintenance Manager for Focus, the reasons for embarking upon BS5750 were

"Firstly was the underlying desire to improve the quality of service to tenants. Secondly, we are increasingly being asked to demonstrate our effectiveness as an organisation to some of our customers ... Thirdly as an amalgamation of three associations, everyone was doing their job but in different ways – we wanted to identify and adopt 'best practice'. BS5750 offered a structure for us to achieve all these aims". (National Federation of Housing Associations 1993 p 19)

Wayne Hughes notes above that Focus has been formed through the merger of three midlands associations and it was this merger that stimulated the push for BS5750. Focus followed the classic implementation route, described earlier and this has meant that they have been able to place their project within a wider customer service strategy. This included greater involvement of front line staff, who experience directly the problems of customer service, in the development of effective procedures. Involvement means greater ownership of the way things should be done and consequently improved team spirit and morale. In addition whilst the project effectively codified existing procedures it also threw up important gaps in procedures. In particular it led to the introduction of procedures to help with continuous improvement. Existing procedures stated what and what not to do, however procedures aimed at identifying errors and rectifying them to prevent re-occurrence had to be created. Focus are now extending their BS5750 programme to other housing management services.

In both these examples there is no evidence that its introduction resulted in the codification of processes which would produce poor quality or services which did not meet expectations. But there is also no evidence that the standards being offered were thoroughly tested with customers. It remains to be seen if these two landlords will be able to easily adjust their repairs services if customers want something different.

Total Quality Management & Customer Service

Selecting TQM

For many organisations a quality assurance system can be an excellent gateway to a quality programme but that is all it is. In developing a model approach which will make a much more powerful contribution to a customer service strategy Total Quality Management is regarded as a much more comprehensive and customer centred approach. Harris Distribution, referred to earlier, looked at several options on how to proceed with quality. They narrowed their choice down to two basic routes.

"We could take either the recognised route of BS5750 or chose the 'attitudinal' route of Total Quality Management." They considered that the two could be combined but that Total Quality must be achieved first. This was because "Total Quality Management emphasises the nature of customers." (Milum 1990, p 57)

Companies that have chosen BS5750 or some other tool as their introduction to quality have often gone on to expand their approach into a fully fledged Total Quality Management programme again to focus their programme more fundamentally on customer service. The international manufacturing group Hilti AG makers of fastening tools, power tools, anchors and construction chemicals, had adopted a fragmented, unstructured approach to the management of total quality. This included the introduction of quality control and quality assurance systems, including BS5750 in the mid 1980's. By 1990, they had shifted to a much more holistic Total Quality Management programme to produce "... a single minded focus on the customer". (Wilshaw, 1990 p 285)

Amongst companies in the service sector where quality control and quality assurance are likely to be less powerful in effectively managing 'moments of truth', the 'attitudual' characteristics of TQM score, and so it is the technique that tends to be selected in the end. This has happened at British Airways and is now happening in the banking and finance sector. In the early 1980's, the National Westminster Bank recognised that customer service would be the important differentiator in the financial services industry, so in 1983 they launched a 'Standards of Service Campaign.' This and subsequent campaigns were variants of traditional customer care programmes. This is a common route into quality and customer service adopted by other banks including the Yorkshire Bank, the Midland Bank and Barclays Bank. By 1987 the National Westminster had expanded their approach into a more wide ranging TQM initiative. The Giro Bank introduced a TQM programme in 1987. It began with 73 specially designed quality workshop training sessions for 3000 employees. They put much of their effort into changing the climate of management. They also introduced quality improvement workshops involving staff from all levels and by 1990 they had registered over 1000 of these workshops. The consultants guiding the Giro Bank noted

> "Today, the Giro Bank process is still based on total quality and is now focused on three key threads of activity : customer care, quality improvement (and) quality assurance." (Memmott, 1991)

The TQM approach is also being promoted as the favoured mechanism for the Health Service. In 1990 the Health Minister, Virginia Bottomley announced a number of demonstration projects to pioneer a TQM approach to health care. She noted with approval the value of TQM as being about

> "... putting patients first – finding out about and satisfying their individual needs and harnessing and developing the talents of every member of staff across all disciplines to the single goal of achieving the best possible standard of health care for their patients." (TQM Magazine 1990, p 255)

As noted earlier, TQM is something of a portmanteau phrase and at its basic level can be little more than an umbrella for the combined use of quality assurance, quality control and other process management systems. As a model approach to enable an organisation to excel at customer service, the variant that experience shows to be the most effective is the one for which the term 'Customer Driven' TQM has been coined.

Let us now look at the key elements of such a model and an example of a housing association that has been working with a variation of it

A 'Customer Driven' TQM model centres on five basic principles

* Culture Change
* Commitment and Leadership
* Customer Focus
* Continuous Improvement
* Cross Functional Teamwork

The approach is to deploy the various quality tools like quality assurance, statistical process control, business process re-design, customer care, benchmarking and so on strictly within this framework of principles. Without this guiding set of principles, the argument goes, the tools can be ill directed and a company will become tool bound rather than customer focused.

Culture Change

Culture can be colloquially defined as "the way we do things around here". Culture change is fundamental to 'Customer Driven' TQM for it proposes, as a pre-requisite to everything else, that the culture of an organisation should be purposefully shifted to one in which how things are organised and how people are managed is wholly driven by the concept of the customer. Working with and applying the quality toolkit listed above helps to define that culture, but at the same time an espoused set of cultural values needs to be clearly posted to ensure these tools remain a means to an end and not an end in themselves. Morris Foster and Susan Whittle of the Change Management Research Unit at Sheffield Business School have described this state as a "Quality Mindset". They argue that

"The challenge ... is to translate the espoused values into a 'taken for granted' set of assumptions shared by everyone. This requires a shift in the focus of change – from the manipulation of systems structures and overt behaviour to a fundamental shake-out in managerial thinking. Culture change means seeing things differently. The task facing managers ... is to learn to see their world from their customers perspective and affect changes that meet the requirements of these perspectives". (Foster et al 1990)

Commitment and Leadership

In many organisations TQM often exists only as a set of espoused values and only held with any conviction by a few quality disciples. To be effective, TQM has to have the total commitment of everybody in the organisation. To get this commitment the managers from the top down must actively lead it. The leadership of a Customer Driven' TQM model requires:

* Inspirational Leadership – in which heartfelt attitudes are developed and nurtured in managers which enables them to focus people on the customer.

* Organisational Leadership – whereby the organisation structures are set up to work around the customer not around a function.

* Situational Leadership – in which managers adapt their style to empower staff to use the full range of quality tools in their daily work.

Customer Focus

The culture change and leadership principles revolve round the concept of the customer as at the centre of everything. In most organisations, this means changing from having an incomplete or ambiguous understanding of customer requirements to a systematic approach to understanding and satisfying both internal and external customers. The importance of becoming obsessed with listening described in detail in the last chapter became one of the important building blocks of 'Customer Driven' TQM. It is this customer focus that provides its distinctive flavour and it is because of this bias that the companies who want to excel at customer service have adopted it.

Customer focus has two strands. First everybody in the organisation must have empathy with the external customer and understand the importance of not just satisfying, but delighting the external customer. Second, the concept of the internal customer – supplier chain needs to be absorbed and made to work. Everybody in the organisation should change from thinking about their roles in terms of static job descriptions listing tasks and responsibilities within a well defined function, to seeing themselves as a customer or supplier in a stream of activity leading to value to the external customer. In organisational terms this means overlaying traditional vertical/functional structures with sets of customer value teams each with their own mission, outputs and customers all locked into a horizontal process chain leading to the external customer. This is particularly important for central service staff such as those in finance or computing who need to see how their bit of work contributes to the organisation's ability to provide value to customers.

Continuous Improvement

In the customer driven quality organisation the objective is to get things right, first time, every time. The acceptance of a certain margin of error which is then put right later has to give way to a striving for defect free products and services achieved by a process of continuous improvement. Thus a target of 98% of repairs completed on time is ultimately not good enough. Only 100% is good enough and then the challenge is to delight the customer by exceeding the expectations. This is achieved by the deployment of problem solving techniques and then corrective processes and measurement tools. In this sense quality and continuous improvement in customer service has to be seen as a never ending journey.

Cross-Functional Teamwork

Natural work groups can achieve a lot in terms of customer focus and problem solving by systematically improving their particular activities. But many problems in any process are due to the failure to manage the gap where a process moves from one work team to another. To tackle this problem, the organisation must enable staff from different functions to come together. For the major business processes that go across several functions, departmental boundaries have to be ignored when seeking to improve them. In a 'Customer Driven' TQM organisation one of the indicators of effective organisational and situational leadership is the willingness of managers to ignore territorial habits. They empower their staff to come together across functions to solve problems, to set up teams to re-design major business processes, or to set up customer orientated strategic business units. Tools like Business Process Re-design require this kind of approach.

Unlike tools such as BS5750, 'Customer Driven' TQM does not prescribe how things should be done. It is not a rigidly defined programme with a beginning and an end that an organisation has to get through. It is a way of working that will take time to implement and will constantly evolve and change. The pages of 'The TQM Magazine' are replete with case studies of different approaches to this kind of TQM and no two approaches are the same. Few companies, particularly service companies, could claim that they have introduced these five principles to maximum effect. Some, like British Airways, have travelled a good way along the route. They have successfully shifted their culture from one dominated by wartime R.A.F. values and the technical pre-eminence of the aircraft, to one dominated by the values of efficient travel and customer service. This has been done using TQM inside the company and customer care with passengers. British Rail claim 'We're Getting There', but here progress is slow. As noted earlier in this book, their early efforts at customer care had limited impact because the culture and focus of the organisation remained firmly engineering and technical, instead of market focused.

TQM Case Study: CCHA Housing

In social housing we have noted that an increasing number of landlords are being drawn into quality through BS5750, although we have no indication that they are considering the attitude approach to customer service enshrined in TQM. Others, noted in earlier chapters, are being drawn into quality management through customer care or by putting the spotlight on broad management values and missions which highlight customer service. Welwyn and Hatfield have launched a number of integrated initiatives including teamworking, quality circles and a customer care programme. East Northamptonshire District Council, York City Council and Coventry City Council have concentrated on the concept of a contract with their customers for one or more services. Orbit Housing Association, Blackburn District Council and Wrekin District Council are other examples of new approaches which pick up on some of the themes and techniques in this model of 'Customer Driven' TQM. But most of these examples indicate that social landlords are where the banks were in the mid 1980's. They are trying to refocus their organisations in a variety of different ways, but they cannot yet claim, and probably do not claim, to be consciously pursuing a 'Customer Driven' TQM programme of the model kind described above.

The approach adopted at CCHA Housing, however, is more closely akin to this TQM model and is positively promoted as such. In the last chapter CCHA's attempts at more sophisticated research into customer expectations through service experience surveys and focus groups were described. These approaches grew out of a specific TQM programme launched in 1990. This programme is one that comes closest to the 'Customer Driven' TQM models used in the private sector.

CCHA decided to go the TQM route rather than the BS5750 or another route because during a period of rapid growth and change they wanted to ensure that quality and personal service did not suffer. They had tried, with limited success, a quality circle approach but they felt a more organisation wide programme was needed. They became aware of TQM through two sources. Two of their suppliers – Rank Zerox and IBM – had well developed TQM programmes which CCHA observed. Also, working in Coventry, they became aware of the TQM initiatives at Rover and Jaguar. This led to an introduction to consultants working out of the CIM Institute at Cranfield Institute of Technology. They had developed a training programme and operational package for a number of manufacturing and service organisations based on the Rank Xerox TQM programme. Working with a project team from CCHA, the consultants adapted it to meet the peculiar needs of social housing. The programme has enabled CCHA to begin to introduce all of the five key principles of 'Customer Driven' TQM – culture change, customer focus, commitment and leadership, cross functional teamwork and continuous improvement. The following approach was adopted:

A Common Definition of Quality

Since quality is one of those words open to many meanings, CCHA believed it was important to have a robust common definition within the organisation. The definition was carefully built to pick out the key elements of the approach which defined quality as, ultimately, what the customer perceived it to be.

So at CCHA quality now means:

"To fully satisfy agreed customer requirements at the lowest internal cost by continually improving our products and services, people and business processes".

Training and Education

The first task was to train all staff from the top down in total quality and the way to work to deliver total quality. The training was carried out on a very structured cascade principle. The top management team was trained first. They went through a four day programme which covered the principles of quality, effective teamworking, problem solving and the wide range of quality tools and techniques that could be deployed. It was action centred training geared around real business problems within CCHA. A crucial part of this training was to build a vision statement for CCHA incorporating a clear mission and a set of culture statements which defined the way the association should do things. These culture statements have proved to be a fundamental guide to ensure the concepts of 'Customer Driven' TQM are understood and promoted.

The organisation was then broken down into natural work teams and each team went through a 3 day training programme. Most managers went through the training twice. Once as a member of a local or departmental management team and then as a team leader of his or her natural work team. Each team followed a similar action centred learning programme covering the ground the top team covered. The main difference was that they had to assess the cultural values defined by the top team on the basis of their importance to CCHA and whether or not the values were at that time weak or strong within CCHA. This process of review now happens every year so that the association can assess progress – as perceived by staff – in building the quality culture espoused. These teams also built local mission statements which meshed with each other and with the overall mission so that every work team could understand at the highest level what they did, why they did it and who they did it for. Again this helped lock each team into a customer value stream in which they began to perceive of their role as a customer or supplier in the overall customer supplier chain leading to the tenant or applicant.

A Support System

It was recognised that in the early years it would be easy for work teams to go through the training but slip back into old ways of doing things under the pressure of everyday problems. Therefore a support network was set up. An executive director was given quality promotion as a major element of his job, a full time co-ordinator was employed and a number of staff were trained as facilitators. These staff kept their normal jobs, but also helped and encouraged work teams with the processes. A facilitator was trained to a higher level of expertise in the tools and processes and they each service one or two work teams usually from a part of the organisation not connected with their natural work area.

The Quality Delivery Process (QDP) and the Quality Improvement Projects (QIP's)

The training was just the start of the programme. The post training activity was to use two team based techniques known as the Quality Delivery Process and Quality Improvement Projects. Each work team is encouraged to go through a continuing ten stage process and – like painting the Fourth Bridge – keep repeating it. The first eight stages comprise the Quality Delivery Process. It enables a team to establish, in a structured way, what they must do to deliver quality. In this mode of operation natural work teams become focused on what they deliver to their customers and how they each add value to the customer value stream. The eight stages involve:

* defining the *mission* of the work team
* determining the key *outputs* of the team
* identifying the *customers*, both internal and external, who receive the outputs
* for each output entering into a dialogue with the customer (using survey, interviewing and focus group techniques) to define and agree *customer requirements* which must be met in order to fully satisfy the customer
* converting requirements into a *specification*
* determining the *processes and procedures* which will deliver the outputs to the customer at the lowest internal cost
* identifying the *measurements* of each output which will compare the actual quality level with the output specification
* identifying any *problems* caused by a measured shortfall to target.

The final two steps form the basis for Quality Improvement Projects. Once a problem has been identified (or an opportunity to exceed a target at no additional cost, or an opportunity to meet customer requirements at a lower internal cost) then a project team is set up to solve the identified problem. Project teams may involve some or all of the natural work team and could include people from other work teams, suppliers or external customers who can help with the problem. Once a solution to a problem has been implemented, customer satisfaction is measured.

Through this rigorous routine, work teams can deploy the full toolkit of quality tools such as statistical process control, (in the measurement and problem identification phase) quality assurance (in the processes and procedures stage), customer research techniques (in the stages involving customer identification, establishing requirements and building a specification), cost of quality analysis and various problem solving techniques such as Pereto analysis, Fishbone analysis and prioritisation.

The routine is rigorous and continuous but the aim in CCHA is to encourage participation rather than force it. A programme of visibly rewarding success by promoting those teams making use of the routines is an integral part of the programme.

TQM at CCHA is still in its infancy compared to the masters of customer service. But the benefits are apparent. The most obvious sign is the completion of over 40 quality improvement projects since the start of the programme. These projects have covered a variety of services provided to internal and external customers including the recruitment of new staff, the reporting of repairs, the allocation of homes, personnel services available to managers, the staff newsletter and internal communication, advice on debt, processing housing benefit and other DSS claims and rent account statements.

It has not always been plain sailing and CCHA has encountered problems in applying TQM. From the problems experienced by CCHA the main lessons are:

*   Pick out the relevant tools from management in manufacturing and the private service sector but be prepared for hostility to the idea of transferring such tools to a social service like a housing association. When using the tools be patient and rigorous. The association suffered, initially, from a rich menu of potential techniques and almost became spoilt for choice. Teams did not always understand and use the tools appropriately.

*   Service quality has to be approached at two different stages; process quality and outcome quality. The Quality Delivery Process and Quality Improvement Projects were very good at tackling process quality but less strong at outcome quality. The outcome value of services as perceived by the customer is now being given a sharper focus.

*   The tackling of problems within natural work teams often meant that organisation wide processes were either ignored or dealt with in departmental pieces. Business Process Re-design has recently been introduced to tackle this area.

* Front line housing management teams took to the process much more readily than central support teams. It is a much harder task to get these central departments to see their administrative routines as internal services and their role as a link in an internal customer supplier chain.

* Some first line managers saw TQM as threatening. Such managers are often the technical experts who spend much time supervising work and dealing with crises. By empowering staff and focusing on prevention and improvement TQM challenged this role. Accordingly effort has had to be directed at shifting the focus of such managers to removing constraints on staff and providing leadership in improving processes with which staff have to work.

* The quality of computer software is crucial for quality of services. In identifying problems in existing processes the importance of information flow and computer software emerged time and time again. The computer department within CCHA has been given a new focus as a Business Systems Department with a major support role in the whole quality programme.

Customer Care and Communication

In delivering the range of housing management services, the employees of a social landlord have to have frequent contact with customers and this brings lots of uncertainty. Housing officers cannot just follow standard instructions, they must make judgements, show initiative and take risks in order to customize service for applicants and occupiers. Service characteristics in housing are not dissimilar to those of an airline or aspects of a bank, building society or shop, in that it places a heavy emphasis on the relationship between customer and worker. If the organisation has each of the other building blocks of an effective customer service strategy described earlier, but the front line staff lack the interpersonal skills to deliver these, the result is service failure. To conclude this chapter let us look at some key approaches to communication and how the careful management of communication – oral and written – can contribute to effective customer service.

Communication is a complex array of skills and signals. To be most effective the communicator needs to use these in harmony so that no individual element is obvious but the message is reinforced by each piece. In doing this, the best at communication adopt a strategy which aims to provide skills in the following core areas

* a demonstration of empathy
* minimising barriers to communication
* defusing threats of violence

* using body language to reinforce the message
* providing effective and fast telephone communication
* ensuring plain language is used in all written communication

Empathy

Empathy, according to Carl Rogers, is "to see the client's world as if it were your own". The central ingredient in this is the ability of a staff member to perceive and communicate accurately and with sensitivity the feelings of the customer. Rather than acting as an observer, the employee must aim to understand the feelings of the customer, from the customer's perspective. In doing this there is no sense of judgement that the customer's views are right or wrong, but that the emotions and reactions are a matter of fact.

To achieve this the employee will need to focus on the customer and their non-verbal communications. These messages may be contradictory, so checking facts with the customer verbally, "that must be very annoying....?", can both confirm emotions and display caring and understanding.

Three core aspects need to be present for a positive outcome to such an interaction; genuineness, non-possessive warmth and active listening. Genuineness means that employees are, as far as possible, completely open with their own feelings. By being in touch with their own emotions they will be more able to manage them, rather than becoming upset or angry in response to the customer's emotional state. They may then choose to share these feelings, or keep them to themselves depending on their judgement of the situation. In displaying non-possessive warmth, the employee must avoid judgement or alignment with the customer's plight. Signals of care and concern must be shown, which reinforce the verbal messages.

Thirdly, the employee must use active listening. Listening is frequently considered to be a passive activity and one in which little thought or action is required. Active listening demands positive action from the employee. They must listen to voice tone, to the specific words which are used, facial expressions and body movements. From this they must decide how to structure their own communication and express their understanding. To achieve this they may seek to combine non verbal communication; eye contact and nods, with verbal attentions; 'yes', 'mmm', 'uh hum', and door openers; 'what', 'where', and 'when'. Finally, they are likely to restate what the customer has said, to clarify meaning and demonstrate understanding.

Minimising Barriers

'The high counters and bare walls made us feel as though we were supplicants at the gates of a Soviet labour camp. There weren't any chairs, I took a number and leaned against a wall to wait my turn.' (Paretsky 1990)

We feel safest behind some kind of physical barrier. But this barrier can increase the isolation of the customer and reduce the effectiveness of the communication.

Our urge to create a barrier to protect ourselves goes back to childhood; the child's efforts to hide behind their parent, or a teenager covering their face in embarrassment. These reactions dwindle as we get older, but are still present in a restricted form in every social interaction, as a fear displacement activity. The more formal the occasion, the more dominant or unfamiliar the individual we are to meet, the more we fear the encounter.

The most common form of body barrier signal is the body cross. In this movement one arm is brought into contact with the other in front of the body. This forms a temporary bar across the chest. The movement may be disguised. In an interview this may take the form of adjusting the watch. Other physical items can form barriers, or ease the feeling of isolation. The employee's decision to take a note pad gives them 'power' over the customer, as does a higher chair and a chair with arms.

Interview barriers in the office environment can be easily and simply reduced by making customers feel the office is an extension of their home. The provision of plants, paintings, toys for the children, soft surfaces and pale colour schemes can assist the customer to feel calm and relaxed. Researchers in the USA have identified from tests that pale pink reduces aggression (The Independent). In highly charged atmospheres the use of recorded subliminal messages has enabled the service supplier to more effectively manage customers. The technique has proved particularly effective in reducing shop lifting, but could equally be applied to reducing violence in benefits or housing offices, as part of a positive strategy to deal with violent customers (Passmore, 1990).

Violence

In the stress of interaction, violence can be an outcome. Two highly publicised deaths, of Harry Collinson and Denis Riley reveal the vulnerability of public sector workers. While we advocate the removal of glass screens and taking down of physical barriers, staff must adopt other techniques for dealing with violence, or this may only add to the risk of attack.

Violence, of course, is more than the single physical attack. It is better defined as an action which is threatening to the individual who is exposed to it. It can range from verbal abuse to threatened violence or actual physical violence.

Customer body language betrays violence and offers signals to staff often before any action or words are said. These threat signals warn of aggression, and staff must be able to interpret and deal with them. Obvious signals such as a pointed figure or, in a seated position, a swung leg indicate aggression and tension. Other subconscious changes in the body may take place, such as skin colour may change as blood flows to the surface. Skill is needed to recognise these signals early, identify the cause and attempt to calm the customer. If the customer is a man, women are usually more effective at doing this, as they are seen as less of a threat.

A precursor to violence may be growing stress. In this instance the violence may be preceded by a dampening down of the usual social processes. This is known as cut-off. This is displayed in the most pronounced way through evasive eye contact; the person may look away for unusually long periods while in conversation. Secondly, the eye contact may be shifty; the person may keep glancing away and back rapidly while in conversation. Thirdly, the eyelid may have spasms of flickering up and down. Alternatively, the eye may stammer, dropping shut for a moment and unable for a second to open. All four actions indicate tension and a wish by the individual to withdraw from the interaction. If this is not possible, or the tension is not eased, violence may develop.

While body language and interpersonal skills are the most effective weapon for reducing the risk of violence, a range of other strategies need to be deployed to compliment the sympathetic stance of the housing officer from the organisation's policies and procedures to the physical environment.

The traditional response is to install screens and suggest incidents are either the result of non-professionalism or are wholly the fault of clients. These viewpoints are over-simplistic. Violence is the end result of an interaction between client and officer which occurs at a specific time and in a specific place (Passmore 1989).

Rather than the traditional negative response a range of positive strategies are available (Passmore 1989). A 'Positive Active' response may include staff training in interview and interpersonal skills. Alternatively, a 'Positive Passive' approach centres on changes to tthe environment which the customer encounters before and during the interview. This includes efforts to alter customer expectations in advance of the interaction through effective publicity, changes to waiting areas, interview rooms. The reception area should be easily identified, the waiting area should be well lit, with adequate space so customers do not feel crowded, surfaces are soft to reduce noise and present an attractive visual appearance. In reception areas where waits may be long the provision of vending machines, soft toys, pay phones and toilets may reduce stress and boredom.

Further, the organisation should be equipped to deal with violence, should it occur; personal alarms, escape doors in interview rooms, self defence training and supportive management which offers thorough recording of incidents, counselling and legal action against attackers.

Body Language

Whether an employee wishes to demonstrate empathy, bring down barriers to communication or defuse threats of violence; body language plays a crucial part. A USA study on communication identified that in deciphering a message the listener, in a face to face encounter, pays greatest attention to body language. Body language makes up 55% of the received communication whilst the other 45% is split 38% voicetone and 7% words. Subconsciously we all use body language to reinforce verbal messages. Skilled communicators can use body language to reinforce a message and to read the messages from their partners in the communication. They may assess whether and how the message is being received and adapt their communication message to assist them in the communication. The objective is to make the individual understand and accept the message. In housing, this is frequently about communicating information the customer does not want to hear. This rarely leads to violence, but customer anger and dissatisfaction are more common.

The aim is to align body language with words and voice tone so that a consistent message is given and reinforced. The simple re-iteration of the message, that the customer's complaint is understood is needed to display empathy. This may be achieved by head nodding and verbal attention – "mmm", "yes", "I understand". To complement this touch may also be used to express understanding. As a result of British cultural barriers to touch, caution is needed in using this technique as touch has strong sexual connotation if used male-female or male-male. As a general rule younger men avoid touch, while older men welcome a formal hand shake. In stressful situations hand to hand, arm or shoulder can signal understanding and support.

Total control over body language, however, is not possible. The human eye can indicate mood changes, over which we cannot exercise control, and of which we are frequently unaware.

The pupil, a black spot at the centre of the iris, narrows in sunlight. At dusk it widens by up to four times its previous diameter. As well as responding to light, the pupil is affected by emotion. It grows larger if we are excited, anticipate pleasure or fear. While lovers may gaze into one another's eyes, the additional eye contact between housing officer and customer may not be totally consistent with the message being given.

Possibly the most useful technique is postural echo, sometimes known as 'mirroring'. We frequently adopt this unconscious union with friends in social situations, sharing body movements to create a carbon copy of each others movements. In friendships there is no need to display power and the individuals are of equal status. The body subconsciously sends the message 'see I'm just like you'. Even when positions change, one friend crosses their leg, the other follows.

Because acting in unison sends a message of equal status and friendship, the housing officer can use it as the dominant individual to put the subordinate at their ease.

Care again has to be taken to not overdo the use of mirroring, as if the copying of movements becomes conscious to the customer it will become irritating and appear patronising.

Telephone Communication

Telephones demand equal, if not greater, communication skills. As both parties are unseen body language is not available to aid our communication. Over the phone, voice tone accounts for 87% of the communication message which the listener receives. Getting this right is thus crucial for effective communication.

Using similar techniques to face to face contact help; verbal attends, summaries and phrases such as "I'm writing this down", all confirm to this listener someone taking an active interest.

The most difficult, and frustrating aspect of telephone communication is the initial contact and reaching the right person. Organisations often neglect to resource the telephonists, so phones ring giving the customer the impression no one cares. The phone should be answered within one and three rings, with the operator giving a greeting and stating the name of the organisation; 'Good afternoon, Institute of Housing'. Having gathered information on who the caller wishes to speak to, the operator should advise the customer they are being 'connected'. However competent the telephonist, large organisations need to ensure staff answer phones quickly, and when they are out divert them to someone who is available to answer them. Here too the individual should give the caller a greeting and their name.

If they need to transfer the call, they need to explain what they are going to do, give the customer the name and number of the person they are transferring them to, inform the other employee of the customers details and finally advise the customer they are being 'connected'.

While apparently simple rules, phone contact with most large local authorities remains a nightmare. It would be nice to think that each reader of this publication ensured their organisation followed these basic rules.

Plain Language

Effective written communication is as important as interpersonal skills. The housing service contacts its customers by letter to inform them of rent increases and benefit calculations, consult them about the management of their home and expects them to fill out forms for everything from a home move to building a shed. Like most organisations, social landlords easily slip into 'bureaucrat ease'. Jargon, long sentences and a general failure to consider the reader dominate. The failure to communicate by the graduate-educated author is seen as a failure of the customer. However, if the author wishes to get a message across, they need to consider the reader and how the message can be delivered so it can be understood. A plain and simple style is likely to be most effective. A set of basic rules has long been advocated. George Orwell set out six elementary rules to improve the clarity of would be writers:

1. Never use a metaphor, simile or other figure of speech which you are used to seeing in print.

2. Never use a long word where a short word will do.

3. If it is possible to cut out a word, always cut it out.

4. Never use the passive where you can use the active.

5. Never use a foreign phrase, a scientific word or a jargon word if you can think of an everyday English equivalent.

6. Break any of these rules sooner than say anything outright barbarous. (Orwell 1946).

Many, however, ignore the reader (PEC 1982) for example:

> "After the acceptance of a housing application, the applicant must immediately notify the Director of Health and Housing if he changes his address or if there is any alteration in his family circumstances. Failure to give such notification will render the application void and it will be deleted from the housing waiting list with little or no prospect of it ever being reinstated thereon".

The letter from Rochford D.C. makes a simple message more complex. While trying to inform customers of the importance of keeping information up to date, the letter seeks to intimidate the reader.

Making a letter simple, but failing to change the style can make things even worse. South Cambridgeshire's approach to rent arrears demonstrates the point.

> "Let me make one thing clear: if for any reason we don't get the money, you'll be out of that house so fast it'll make your head spin and we won't be rehousing you" (PEC 1982).

The Plain English Campaign have produced a measure for assessing the difficulty of adult reading material. The FOG index is based on sentence length and word length. The longer sentences or words, the higher the FOG factor. As a comparison The Sun has an average FOG factor of 26, the Guardian 39. Most legal documents, and the letters above fall into the 40-60 bracket. At 40 the document is a struggle for The Sun reader, at 60 the Guardian reader struggles (NCC 1983).

A more customer friendly style can be achieved, while still keeping the letter plain and simple. Five guiding rules can be applied:

---

* avoid jargon

* use active verbs

* avoid sentences longer than 15 words

* use positive words/phrases

* use a pleasant tone

Jargon is a feature of housing, as of any other profession. When communicating between professionals it proves an effective shorthand; LSVT or CCT rather than Large Scale Voluntary Transfer or Compulsory Competitive Tendering save time and effort. These and other terms, however, provide a barrier when communicating with non-professionals.

As well as specialist phrases, Latin and French phrases also generate complexity and failure to understand; prima facie, ipso facto, and mutatis mutandis place non grammar school readers at a disadvantage. In producing correspondence, the author needs to ask the simple questions; who is the reader?, what am I trying to say?, what am I trying to get them to do? The answers to these three questions will affect the letter's style and content.

The second aspect to consider is the need to use active verbs. Public sector organisations have become masters of using passive verbs. These letters sound as if a machine is communicating with another machine. They lack the personal touch. In technical terms the difference between passive and active verbs is in the sentence structure. The switch from passive to active is simple, and can be combined with an effort to make the correspondence more personal. This means replacing "It is regretted that your husband has passed away", with "I am sorry to hear of your husband's death". By clearly stating who the agent is, a more personal tone can be given.

Thirdly, use short sentences. Long sentences are difficult to write, as the author risks ambiguity and the relationship between other ideas becomes confused. Readers can forget the meaning by the end of the sentence, which runs to 50 or more words. Sentences of 15 words are most suited to ease of understanding, with each idea having its own sentence.

Fourthly, readers find positive instructions easier to understand than negative ones.

> "You must not paint your Council dwelling without the prior permission of the Council".

> "You must get our agreement before painting your home".

The final guideline is adjusting the tone of the letter to suit the customer and the message. In many instances a staff member will be replying to an enquiry from a customer and may use their writing skills as a guide to the tone and scope of the reply. Where the letter is going to many or an unknown reader, a simple polite and personal style may be preferred. However, avoid being patronising; no one likes being treated as a 12 year old.

As well as the words used in letters and forms, presentation too has a great impact. The following guidelines apply to most publications (Housing 1991):

* typeface – 10 point as a minimum
* plenty of white space
* use graphics and tables where appropriate to explain statistics
* structure the content
* emphasise important sections or headings

Effective communication is a fundamental attribute of any customer service strategy and is an important element in any customer driven quality programme. Good service design and quality assured processes are no good without effective customer care and effective communication strategies; the obverse also holds true. K. James has succinctly drawn out the importance of the integrated nature of these elements in quality management.

> "A housing department reports an incident in which an angry interchange had occurred between a husband and wife, who had come to get some repairs done to their house, with the person on the desk. The clerk had entered their request on the terminal and told the couple that they would be notified when the repair would be done. The couple had asked when this would be, but since the information was stored on the mainframe, which could not be interrogated from the office, the clerk had explained she was not able to tell them …. The couple clearly thought she was fobbing them off and were getting irate... The clerk dealt with the situation as best she felt fit, coolly repeating that she could not give the information out and that they would be informed in due course". James (1989)

The housing repairs case demonstrates how failure of support service back-up, in this case of information provided by IT, can prevent an integrated service being provided. No matter how skilful the interpersonal skills of the clerk, the customers expected information about their repair which the clerk could not provide.

The growth in customer service techniques which seek in part to manipulate customer feelings to generate satisfaction and improved image or profit, place a great burden on those expected to perform.

In some sectors the expectations are particularly high, where competition is strong and differentiation of services relies on the personal interaction. Airline services are a classic example and one in which organisations such as British Airways and Singapore Airlines compete on service quality rather than price or technical service quality such as newer or faster planes. Instead flight attendants are seen as the differentiation factor. While not explicit, business travellers are tempted to travel by the sexy image of attendants. The reality of travel is very different and attendants can't live up to the fantasy of advertising despite training which suggests that the customer is never wrong. Instead "in a near-

Orwellian Newspeak", the company seems to have officially eliminated the very idea of getting angry at the passenger ..... "Supervisors never speak of an obnoxious passenger or outrageous passenger, only of an uncontrolled passenger .... or ..... mishandled passenger." Hochchild (1983).

For the employee of a social landlord the dilemma of managing customer feelings is even more difficult. On one hand is a wish to see customers satisfied with the service and to meet customer expectations and demands. On the other hand is the need to enforce tenancy conditions, ration housing allocations and reject some homeless applicants. One suggests a need for a subservient approach of the 'customer is always right', the second suspicion of customer motives and attention to the facts and legal obligations. The employer expects the housing officer to act both roles, swopping identities as customers housing problems presented to them at the desk change.

Should employers hold such expectations? Is this act sustainable, or will the cracks in the technique of emotion management reveal the truth to the customers who are becoming increasingly presented with 'smile' treatment? Unless staff do care about the service they provide and the customers whom they serve, we fear techniques will be insufficient to demonstrate a customer service culture.

Such care is best demonstrated not by learned techniques, although if used effectively they ease personal conflict, but by innovation. The employee who performs the service not to the letter of the housing management contract or customer charter, but adapts the service to meet the challenges which customers present every day to customer contact staff. To respond, staff need to understand the organisation, its mission and have the freedom to act to find the appropriate solution there and then.

Quality Programmes and Customer Service

It has been our purpose in these last two chapters to describe in some detail the way private companies, and particularly the private service companies, have approached the issue of customer service. Most organisations who have become masters of customer service have done so by completely changing their whole business strategy. In chapter seven, the main theme was that one key strand in this strategy is their obsession with listening and the deployment of sophisticated market research techniques to enable them to understand their customers expectations. The theme of this chapter is that the same companies also put in place some kind of quality management programme to enable them to respond to those expectations. In applying quality management techniques, service companies have used tools developed in manufacturing but in adapting and using them some important lessons need to be observed.

In the changing world of social housing where competitive advantage is beginning to loom large, the experience of the private sector is a valuable one to observe, learn from and adapt. Even without the pressure of competition the provision of social housing and the associated housing management service ought to be driven not by politics, or cost or the size of the development programme but by the customer and customer service.

Summary

- There are a whole raft of quality tools derived from manufacturing. Even the most product centred like Quality Function Deployment can be adapted to suit services. However they need to be used carefully and selectively. Many are only suited to tackle the control of processes before a service is actually delivered; and these do not tackle the 'moments of truth' of service interaction.

- Since most quality programmes are tool based, it is easy to become tool bound. This is particularly a danger if the organisation has a quick fix mentality and is looking for an heroic solution to their quality problems. Quality programmes are a never ending journey – a way of managing not a programme you go through.

- A quality programme as a means to improved customer service can be launched in a number of different ways. Quality Circles, BS5750 and Customer Care are common entry points and this has certainly been the experience of many social landlords. However, other service providers who started in this way invariably move onto the more holistic TQM approach which draws all the tools together and puts the customer at the centre. There are a number of variations to TQM, but the most powerful in support of a customer service strategy is the one described here as 'Customer Driven' TQM with its four guiding principles of culture change, customer focus, commitment and leadership, cross functional teamwork and continuous improvement.

- However well designed the services and effective the quality assured procedures, customer satisfaction often hangs on the hundreds of 'moments of truth' when the customer communicates with the organisation. Such 'moments of truth' have to be controlled through a managed approach to communication whether face to face, by telephone or in writing. In the end, the customers of a housing association or a local authority want the same things as the customers of British Airways, who were concerned with how spontaneous the flexible BA employees were in applying company policies and with their ability to recover from mistakes by making things right for the passenger (L Bruce, 1987).

REFERENCES

Chapter 1:

Commission for Racial Equality (1991), 'Code of Practice on Rented Housing'.

Department of Health (1991), 'The patients' Charter', HMSO.

Friends of the Earth (1989), 'The Environmental Charter – For Local Government – practical Recommendation'.

National Council for Voluntary Organisations (1984), 'Clients' Rights: Report of an NCVO Working Party', Bedford Square Press.

Page, D. (1993), 'Building Communities', Joseph Rowntree Trust (*).

Passmore, J. (1992), 'Who cares wins', Housing October (*).

Key Readings are marked with an *.

Chapter 2:

ADC/IOH (1993), 'Competition and Local Authority Housing Services: A guidance manual', ADC/IOH.

Berry P. (1991), 'The Customer is King, Long Live the Citizen', Going Local, Spring 1991.

Donaldson L. (1993), 'Chartering a Hotline for the Citizen', The Independent 25th February 1993 pp16.

HMSO (1992a), 'Council Tenants' Charter'.

HMSO (1991), 'The Citizens' Charter', CM 1599, July 1991 (*).

HMSO (1992), 'The Citizens' Charter: First Report', CM 2101, November 1992.

Niner P. (1992), 'Making the Best of Performance Reports', Inside Housing, 14th August 1992 page 8-9.

Passmore J. (1991a), 'Flawed Performance by DOE', Housing, March 1991.

Passmore, J. (1991b), 'Inadequacy of Top Down Style', Public Finance and Accountancy, March 1991.

Passmore, J. (1990), 'Customer Care – Cultural Change at Welwyn Hatfield', Local Government Studies, September/October 1990.

Seabrook, J. (1984), 'The Idea of Neighbourhood', Pluto Press, London (*).

Key readings are marked with an *

Chapter 3:

Duncan, R. (1977), 'Strategies for Planned Change', John Wiley, New York.

Kotter, J. and Schlesinger, L. (1979), 'Choosing Strategies for Change', Harvard Business Review, March/April 1979. (*)

Newman and Wallender (1983), 'Managing not for Profit Enterprises', in 'The Management Process: a Selection of Readings', Librarians Pearson Red American Library Association, Chicago, Illinois.

Orbit Housing Association (1992), 'Strategy for the 1990s', January 1992.

Passmore, J. (1990), 'Customer Care – Cultural Change at Welwyn Hatfield', Local Government Studies, September/October 1990.

Perrow, C. (1961), 'The Analysis of Goals in Complex Organisations', American Sociological Review, Vol 26, December 1961.

Pugh, D. (1978), 'Understanding and managing organisational change', London Business School Journal, Vol. 3, No. 2. (*)

Richards, T. (1983), 'Making New Things Happen', Technovation, Vol. 3.

Roof (1993), 'Priority Homeless Lettings by the Twenty Biggest Housing Associations', March/April 1993.

Shelter (1993), 'Summary of Shelter's Plans', Internal Document.

Key readings are marked with an *

Chapter 4:

Guest, D. (1982), 'Right enough to be dangerously wrong', in "Human Resource Strategies", ed. Salaman, G., sage (*)

Hambleton, R. (1990), 'Urban Government in the 1990s: Lessons from the USA', SAUS Occasional Paper 3. (*)

Handy, C. (1976), 'Understanding Organisations', Penguin.

Handy, C. (1989), 'The Age of Unreason', London. (*)

Hertzberg, F. (1966), 'Work and the Nature of Man', World Publishing Co.

Kanter, R. (1983), 'The Change Masters', Unwin Hyman.

Mintzberg, H. (1979), 'The Structure of Organisations', Prentice Hall.

Peters, T. (1988), 'Thriving on Chaos', MacMillian London.

Peters, T. (1992), 'Liberation Management', MacMillian London.

Peters, T. and Austin, N. (1985), 'A Passion for Excellence', New Year Random House.

Peters, T. and Waterman, R. (1982), 'In Search of Excellence – Lessons from America's Best Run Companies', Harpers and Row. (*)

Rigby, R. (1982), 'Residents as a Resource – A Public Housing Management Demonstration in Jersey City', Bollinger Press, Cambridge.

Rigby, R. (1989), 'Revitalising Distressed Public Housing: A Management Case', paper presented to NAHRO (US) International Conference, October 1989.

Seabrook, J. (1984), 'The Idea of Neighbourhood', Pluto Press. (*)

Schumacher, E. (1973), 'Small is Beautiful: Economics as if People Mattered', Harper and Row, New York. (*)

Weber, M. (1947), 'The Theory of Social and Economic Organisation', trans by Henderson, A. R. and Parsons, T., London, William Hodge.

Key readings are marked with an *

Chapter 5:

Blake, J., 'The Unnamed Ombudsman', Inside Housing, 26 February 1993. (*)

Braintree, D. C. (1992), 'Total Management – Statement of Management Approach', Braintree, Internal Document.

Braintree, D. C. (1992), 'Housing Matters – Housing Management and Rural Housing Initiative', Braintree, Internal Document.

Camfield B. (1990), 'Putting the Customer First', Management Education and Development, Vol 21.

Clarke, M. and Stewart, J. (1986), 'The Public Service Orientation – Developing the Approach', Local Government Training Board.

Clarke, M. and Stewart, J. (1987), 'The Public Service Orientation – Developing the Approach', Local Government Policy Making, Vol. 13, No. 4, March 1987.

Hambleton, R. (1991), 'Beyond Customer Care', Going Local, Spring 1991.

Hambleton, R. and Hogget, P. (1990), 'Beyond Excellence – Quality Local Government in the 1990s', Working Paper 85, SAUS. (*)

Hancox, A. et al (1988), 'The Wrekin Approach', Local Government Studies, 1988 (*)

Housing Association Weekly, 'Complaints System Fails Tenants', 12 July 1991.

Housing Corporation (1993), 'Resolving Housing Association Complaints'.

Institute of Housing (1993), 'Standards for Housing Management'. (*)

Islington LBC (1993), 'Housing Plans for Islington's Future – Commitments'.

Kettleborough, H. (1988), 'Close to the customer – A well woman approach', Local Government Studies, September/October 1988.

Labour Party (1991), 'NEC Action/Advice Note – Citizens' Charter', Circular No. 11/91 July 1991.

Maud, J. (1976), 'Committee on the Management of Local Government', HMSO.

Miller, K. (1989), 'Pleasing Apologies', Local Government Chronical, 15 December 1989.

Muller, F. (1991), 'A New Engine of Change in Employee Relations', Personnel Management July 1991.

National Consumer Council (1991), 'Housing Complaints Procedure – Principles of good practice for social landlords'.

Passmore, J. (1991), 'A Passion for Customers', Local Government Policy Making, Vol. 18, No. 2.

Phillips, S. (1992), 'Tenants Together – Tenant Participation and Council Housing', TPAS/PEP/DOE.

Pollitt, C. (1990), 'Doing Business in the Temple – Managers and quality Assurance in the Public Services', Public Administration, Winter 1990.

Potter, J. 'Consumerism and the Public Sector: How well does the coat fit', Public Administration, Vol. 86, Winter 1990.

Richards, J. (1992), 'Performance Indicators', Housing March 1992.

Rhodes, R. (1987), 'Developing the Public Service Orientation', Local Government Studies, May/June 1987. (*)

Seneviratne, M. and Cracknell, S. (1988), 'Consumer complaint in public sector services', Public Administration Vol. 66, No. 2.

Smith, R. and Walker, R. (1993), 'An Evaluation of Welsh Housing Management Performance Indicators Regime', Papers in Housing Management and Development No. 7, University of Wales.

Stewart, J. and Clarke, M. (1985), 'Local Government and the Public Service Orientation or Does a Public Service Provide for the Public?' Local Government Training Board, August 1985.

Stewart, J. and Clarke, M. (1987), 'The Public Service Orientation: What is meant by the Public Service Orientation', Local Government Policy Making, March 1986. (*)

Van Gunsteren, H. (1987), 'Notes on the Theory of Citizenship', in Birnboum, P., Lively, J. and Perry, G. (ed), 'Democracy Consensus and Social Contract', Sage.

Wille, E. (1992), 'Quality Achieving Excellence', Ashridge.

Key readings are marked with an *

Chapter 6:

ADC/IOH (1993), 'Competition and Local Authority Housing Services: a guidance manual', ADC/IOH.

Kanter, R. and Summer, D. (1987), 'Doing Well While Doing Good: Dilemmas of Performance Measurement in Non-Profit Organisations and the Need for Multiple Consistency Approach', in Powell, W. 'The Non-Profit Sector – A Research Handbook', Yale University Press. (*)

Passmore, J. (1992), 'Who Cares Wins', Housing, October 1992.

Key readings are marked with an *.

Chapter 7:

Albrecht K. and Zembe R. (1985), 'Service America', Warner Books.

Asher, M. (1989), 'Measuring Customer Satisfaction', The TQM Magazine; Feb 1989.

Bruce, L. (1987), 'British Airways Jolts Staff with a Cultural Revolution', International Management March, 1987.

Carlzon J. (1987), 'Moments of Truth', Ballinger.

Catterick P. (1992), 'Total Quality : An Introduction to Quality Management in Social Housing'. Institute of Housing.

Citizen's Charter (1992), 'First Report'. HMSO.

Citizen's Charter (1993) 'Charter Mark Scheme 1993. Guide for Applicants'. HMSO.

Davey, P. (1993), 'Dealing with Complaints and Compensation'. National Federation of Housing Associations.

Davidow W. and Uttal B. (1989). 'Total Customer Service'. Harper Collins.

Eleftheriades S. (1993) 'Derby D C Customer Panels', Housing Sept 1993.

Goodman, J. A. (1986) 'Consumer Complaint Handling in America. An Update Study for the US Office of Consumer Affairs', Technical Assistance Research Programmes Institution Washington 1986.

Hedges, A. (1990) 'Qualitative Survey among CCHA Residents'. CCHA Housing.

Heskett, J. L. (1986), 'Managing in the Service Economy'. Harvard Business School Press

Housing Corporation (1992). 'Performance Audit Visit Manual'. Housing Corporation

INLOGOV (1982) 'Register of Local Authorities' Research Projects', University of Birmingham.

Joseph Rowntree Memorial Trust (1990), 'Search: Recent Work of the Joseph Rowntree Memorial Trust'. Joseph Rowntree Foundation.

Line, R. (1992), 'Peering Down into the Coalface', Housing, November 1992.

Luthans, F. (1991), 'Improving the Delivery of Quality Service: Behavioural Management Techniques', Leadership and Organisation Development Journal, Vol. 12, No. 2, 1991.

Mistra, A. (1985), 'A Guide to Tenant Surveys'. Paddington Churches Housing Association.

Moore, M. (1992), 'Taking One Step Beyond Quality', Management Consultancy May 1992.

National Federation of Housing Associations (1992), 'Improving Your Use of Performance Indicators'. National Federation of Housing Associations.

Nyquist, J. D., Bittnere, M. J. and Booms, B. H. (1985) 'Identifying Communication Difficulties in the Service Encounter. A Critical Incident Approach', in Czeprel, J. A., Solomon, M. R. and Surprenant, C. F., The Service Encounter. Lexington Books.

Prescott-Clarke, P., Atkins, J. and Clemens, S. (1993) 'Tenant Feedback: A Step-by-Step Guide to Tenant Satisfaction Surveys'. HMSO.

Seviour, D. (1993), 'A Place on the Panel', Housing April 1993.

Trade and Industry, Department (1989). 'Best Practice Benchmarking'. Department of Trade and Industry.

Zeithaml, V. A., Parasuraman, A. and Berry, L. L. (1985) 'A Conceptual Model of Service Quality and its Implications for Future Research' Journal of Marketing, 49, 1985.

Chapter 8:

ADC/IOH (1993), 'CCT Housing Management Guidance Manual' ADC.

Atkinson, P.E. (1990), 'Creating Culture Change: The Key to Successful Total Quality Management' IFS Publications.

Bruce, L. (1987), 'British Airways Jolts Staff with a Cultural Revolution', International Management March 1987.

Catterick, P. (1992) 'Total Quality: An Introduction to Quality Management in

Social Housing'. Institute of Housing.

Cooper Bassett, (1993), 'BS5750: A Survey of Current Housing Authority Activity' Cooper Bassett.

Cooper Bassett, (1993) 'Newsletter', Summer 1993 and Autumn 1993.

Cults M. and Maher C. (1982), 'Gobbledygook', Allen and Unwin.

Dale, A. and Wooler, S. (1990), 'Strategy and Organisation for Service' in Brown, S. W. et al (eds) 'Quality in Services: Multidisciplinary and Multinational Perspectives', Lexington Books.

Davidow, W. and Uttal, B. (1989), 'Total Customer Service', Harper Collins.

Davies, P (1992), 'Perspectives: A Timely Reminder', The TQM Magazine August 1992.

Deming, W. E. (1988), 'Out of Crises', Cambridge University Press.

Economist (1991), 'Style Guide', Business Books.

Edwards, S. and Smith, S. (1989) 'Banking on Total Quality', The TQM Magazine, February 1989.

Ferguson, I. (1990), 'Process Design', The TQM Magazine, April 1990.

Foster, M. and Whittle, S. (1989), 'The Quality Maze' The TQM Magazine, May 1989.

Foster, M. and Whittle, S. (1990), 'Quality – It's All in the Mindset', The TQM Magazine, February 1990.

George, W. R. and Gibson, B. E, (1990), 'Blue-printing: A Tool for Managing Quality in Service' in Brown, S. W. et al (eds) 'Quality in Services: Multidisciplinary and Multinational Perspectives', Lexington Books.

Goodstalt, P. (1990), 'Exceeding Customer Expectations' The TQM Magazine, April 1990.

Gummerson, F. (1990), 'Service Design', The TQM Magazine, April 1990.

Halliday, S. (1993), 'More on the BS5750 fiasco', The Observer, 18 April 1993.

Hammer, M. and Champy J. (1993), 'Re-engineering the Corporation: A

Manifesto for Business Revolution', Brealey Publishing.

Hochchild, A. (1983) 'The Management Heart: Commercialization of Human Feelings', University of California Press.

Housing Management Advisory Panel for Wales (1992) 'Right First Time: Introducing Quality in Housing Services', Housing Management Advisory Panel for Wales.

Housing (1991), 'Producing an Annual Report on Management Performance' Housing, April 1991.

Independent (1993), 'Drivers to see Pink in Soothing Slough', Independent, 15 March 1993.

James, K. (1989) 'Encounter Analysis: Front Line Conversations and their Role in Improving Customer Service', Local Government Studies, May/June 1989.

Kanter, R, and Summers D, (1987) 'Doing Well While Doing Good: Dilemmas of Performance Measurement in Non-Profit Organisations and the Need for Multiple Consistency Approach', in Powell, W. The Non-Profit Sector: A Research Handbook Yale, University Press.

MacDonald, J. (1992), 'Reasons for Failure' The TQM Magazine, August 1992.

Memmott, D. (1991), 'Investing in Change', The TQM Magazine, October 1991.

Milum, K. (1990) 'Commitment to Service Excellence', The TQM Magazine, February 1990.

Moore, M. (1992), 'Taking One Step Beyond Quality', Management Consultancy, May 1992.

National Federation of Housing Associations (1993) 'BS5750: A Tool for Improvement', National Federation of Housing Associations.

NCC/Cults M. and Maher C. (1983),'Small Print: Report to the National Consumer Council', NCC.

Neave, H. R. (1990), 'Why SPC', British Deming Association.

Nichols, J. (1990) 'Value to the Customer' The TQM Magazine, April 1990.

Nicholls J. (1992), 'Leadership of Customer Driven TQM: A Handbook for Managers', (Letchworth Technical Communications).

Orwell, G. (1946), 'Politics and the English Language'.

Paretsky, S. (1990), 'Burn Marks', Virago.

Passmore, J. (1989) 'Violent Clients', Housing and Planning Review, April/May 1989.

Passmore J. (1991), 'How to cope with Violence' Housing and Planning Review, August/September 1991.

Peters, T. and Austin, N. (1986) 'A Passion for Excellence'.

Peters, T. (1988), 'Thriving on Chaos'.

Plain English Campaign (1986), 'The Plain English Story', Plain English Campaign.

Smith, S. (1989), 'Perspectives: Trends in TQM' The TQM Magazine, February 1989.

TQM Magazine (1989), 'The Service Sector responds to the Quality Challenge'.

TQM Magazine (1990) 'Quality at Work', October 1990.

Van trappen, A. (1992) 'Creating Customer Value by Streamlining Business Processes', Long Range Planning, vol. 25, No. 1, 1992.

Wilshaw, G. and Bale, D. (1990) 'Hilti Sells Total Quality', The TQM Magazine, October 1990.

Woodcock, C. (1992), 'The Cost of Keeping Up to Standard', The Guardian, August 31 1992